Twelve and a Tilly

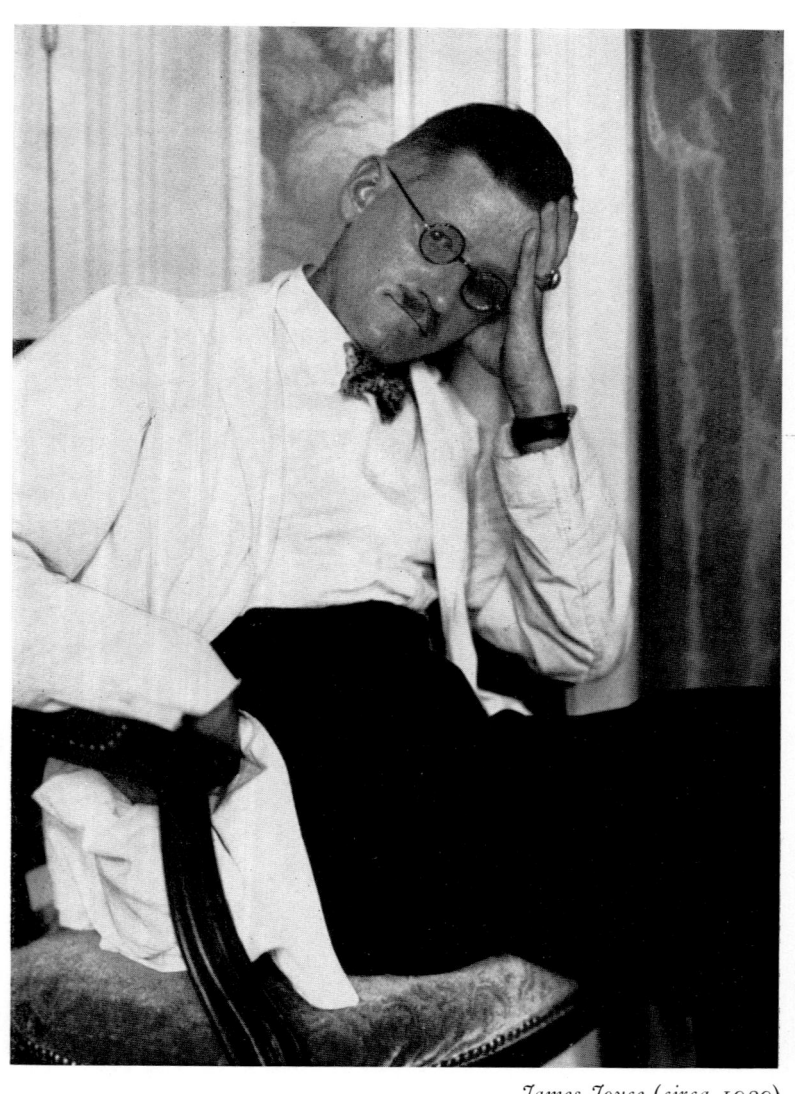

James Joyce (circa 1929)

Twelve and a Tilly

*Essays on the Occasion of
the 25th Anniversary of
Finnegans Wake*

edited by
JACK P. DALTON and
CLIVE HART

NORTHWESTERN UNIVERSITY PRESS
Evanston 1965

Printed in Great Britain

© 1966 by *Jack P. Dalton and Clive Hart*
Library of Congress Catalog Card Number: 65-27700

Contents

IN MEMORY OF JAMES JOYCE Padraic Colum	page 9
RESURRECTION Frank Budgen	11
'THE SEIM ANEW': FLUX AND FAMILY IN 'FINNEGANS WAKE' Frederick J. Hoffman	16
JAMES JOYCE AND THE MACARONIC TRADITION Vivian Mercier	26
INSECTS APPALLING Fritz Senn	36
BYRON IN 'FINNEGANS WAKE' Robert F. Gleckner	40
SPORT AND GAMES IN 'FINNEGANS WAKE' James S. Atherton	52
ON TEACHING 'FINNEGANS WAKE' J. Mitchell Morse	65
THE DATE OF EARWICKER'S DREAM Nathan Halper	72

5

'NOTHING ODD WILL DO LONG': SOME THOUGHTS ON
'FINNEGANS WAKE' TWENTY-FIVE YEARS LATER   page 91
    Richard M. Kain

USES OF THE 'FINNEGANS WAKE' MANUSCRIPTS   99
    A. Walton Litz

'SCRIBBLEDEHOBBLES' AND HOW THEY GREW: A TURNING
POINT IN THE DEVELOPMENT OF A CHAPTER   107
    David Hayman

ADVERTISEMENT FOR THE RESTORATION   119
    Jack P. Dalton

References   138

The Contributors   139

Editorial Afterword   141

Acknowledgments

Acknowledgments and thanks are due to the following:

New Directions for permission to quote from *Stephen Hero* by James Joyce, edited by Theodore Spencer, John J. Slocum and Herbert Cahoon, also to the Executors of the James Joyce Estate and Jonathan Cape.

Jonathan Cape for permission to quote from *A Portrait of the Artist as a Young Man*, also to the Viking Press Inc., their edition copyright 1916 by B. W. Huebsch, 1944 by Nora Joyce, copyright 1964 by the Estate of James Joyce.

Random House and the Bodley Head Ltd. for permission to use material from *Ulysses* by James Joyce, the Random House edition copyright 1914, 1918 and renewed 1942, 1946 by Nora Joseph Joyce.

Faber and Faber Ltd. and the Viking Press Inc. for permission to use extracts from *Finnegans Wake* by James Joyce.

The Dolmen Press, Dublin, for permission to use the poem by Padraic Colum which previously appeared as *The Artificer* in his *Irish Elegies*, copyright 1958, 1961.

To the University of Tulsa (Oklahoma) for *Advertisement for the Restoration* which is partly a rewriting of two articles that originally appeared in the *James Joyce Quarterly*, volume 1, nos. 2 and 3 (1964).

IN MEMORY OF JAMES JOYCE

The long flight and asylum barely reached –
Asylum, but no refuge from affliction
That bore on you and left you helpless there –
That was the word was brought me: loneliness
That was small portion of the loneliness
That days and nights was with you, came to me.

Dedalus! Has your flight ended so?

I looked back to the days of our young manhood,
And saw you with the commons of the town,
Crossing the bridge, and you
In odds of wearables wittily worn,
A yachtsman's cap to veer you to the seagulls,
Our commons also, but your trafficking –
For sum your books would get along the Quay.

And then, with shillings flushed,
To Barney Kiernan's for the frothy pints
And talk that went with porter-drinkers there.
But you
Are also Schoolman, and these casual men
Are seen, are held by you in circumstance
Of history; their looks, their words
By you affirmed, will be looked back on,
Will be rehearsed. Nor they, nor I,
Nor any other will discern in you
The enterprise that you in secrecy
Had framed – to soar, to be the man with wings.

We did not know
The searching eyes beneath the peak of cap
Beheld

The Seventh City of Christendom
Re-famed. We did not know
Below your sayings there was incantation
To give the river back to twilit field,
River of discourse,
                    Anna Livia,
River of fable,
                    Plurabelle.
PADRAIC COLUM

Frank Budgen

RESURRECTION

I am not the ideal reader, and in spite of an average sort of uneasy conscience and noises in the street, I sleep well. With these handicaps I was faced with *Finnegans Wake* at a time before keys were made to fit all its locked doors. Therefore I had to look around for some sort of Ariadne thread spun out of such yarn as was available, and trust to it to guide me at least part of the way through the labyrinth.

The first strand in my thread was that passage in *Stephen Hero* where Stephen ruminates on writing a book on 'the twin eternities of spirit and nature' expressed 'in the twin eternities of male and female'. As soon as I read that I jumped to the conclusion that this was the germ idea of *Finnegans Wake*.

As it stands, Stephen's idea is just another piece of abstract philosophical speculation—about as little fitted for poetic treatment as any grain of mustard seed for human consumption. And yet, and yet the fact that the idea was Dublin-born conferred upon it a certain survival-value and a definite priority. Something in Joyce's inner and outer experience called the seed to life, and something in the climate of European thought in the early twenties fostered its growth.

There is no natural law that proclaims a plant must resemble the seed out of which it sprang. But given male and female—eternal or mortal—and what more likely than a family? And for the urban poet the family must have a city for its activities and fellowships. No need in this case to ask which city. And then the poet, being what he is, must inevitably include in his composition an objectified figure of himself, complete with its opposite numbers.

So far this would be just the mixture as before. But this pair, besides being recognisably human, are also eternal elements shaping and re-shaping the pattern of human existence. Where put them so that they may manifest themselves as both? Joyce's solution, a stroke of genius, was to make them free of the mock eternity of sleep. And, further, in order to sustain the double character of his personages, he provided them with forms of action and modes of speech appropriate to their occasions, borrowed from the Nomansland of dreams lying between sleep and waking, for, as I see it, neither deep sleep nor death has any speech to offer.

Joyce once told me (it was during the composition of *Finnegans Wake*) that he thought he had found the meaning of the Tower of Babel story. If I had done my bounden duty I should have been ready with 'what?' and 'how?' and 'tell', but, slow of wit and more apt to ruminate than ask, I let the occasion slide, so that what Joyce thought was the true inwardness of the Biblical story is anybody's guess.

I wonder if Joyce saw the Plain of Shinar and its presumptuous builders as existing in a world of the collective unconscious. Their tower then would be a sort of Hegelian tower of knowledge starting from nothing and stretching to the comprehension of everything—built, however, not with man-made categories but with pure *a priori* intuitions. In that case, waking them out of their Paradise to the 'real world' of time and space, subject and object, perception and its limitations would suffice to confuse and scatter them.

'Dies is Dorminus master . . .'

So much for the twin eternities of spirit and nature expressed in the twin eternities of male and female. A rather slender thread, it may be thought, and one more likely to bog me down in some private little gnosis of my own than to lead me through the maze of *Finnegans Wake*.

But I had another and stronger strand to my thread, and one sanctioned by Joyce himself. He once told me (no doubt others too) that *Finnegans Wake* was a Resurrection Myth. This seemed to me at first to make everything plain sailing, and so, up to a point, it did. But I began to ask myself, what sort of resurrection? Who or what is it that dies and is reborn? For, if we come to think of it, belief in a resurrection of some sort or other is about the only belief that all human beings of all places and all times have held in common.

The Norse warrior had his Valhalla where the earthly round of eating, drinking and fighting went on until Ragnarok. The same with the Red Indian in his Happy Hunting Grounds, and the ancient

Egyptian, united with Osiris, did in heaven what he loved to do on earth. Saint Paul envisaged the souls of the faithful as receiving an incorruptible body, but, unlike the others, he did not describe the souls' pursuits in heaven. However much these conceptions differ in height and depth, they seem to me to have one thing in common: their pattern follows a straight line from birth through death to the life beyond.

But of what nature is the resurrection in *Finnegans Wake*?

If I am right, and *Finnegans Wake* is the story of the twin eternities of spirit and nature expressed in the twin eternities of male and female, then, as I see it, only one of the twin eternities suffers death and is reborn. That is of course Anna Livia Plurabelle – as woman, as man born of woman, as mother nature, as body, as any body, as all things that appear and live and pass away. She is *das ewig Weibliche* and also *alles Vergängliche*. She has lain the life long night with her partner, but at daybreak they part company. She leaves his bed to go forth by day alone, and only she suffers the agony of parting.

Meanwhile he, the male, the spiritual element, indifferent to her agony – leaving, so to speak, the dead to bury the dead – is intent only upon meeting and mating with a daughter bride coming down to him from the hills.

'Sonhusband' she calls him in her swansong between Chapelizod and the sea. Why 'sonhusband' if both are twin eternities? It reverses in any case the priority given in the Book of Genesis. It might express, probably does in a minor way, any wife's way of looking at any husband – as a boy to be cosseted and scolded and as a man to be looked up to as a provider and protector. There is also a slight hint of an Oedipus-Jocasta relationship, but I feel quite sure that this was not intended. Anyway, the parallel does not hold good. I think rather the explanation is that whilst *nous*, mind, spirit, the male principle is co-eternal with matter, it is, in the time-order of manifestation as self-conscious mind, a late arrival. Anna Livia, nature, must die and be re-born continually. He renews himself through constant remarriage with nature renewed.

The river was born at a certain place as a drop of water fallen from her mother's blue bedroom, the sky, and she meets her end in the arms of her cold grey feary father, Ocean. Her lover and sonhusband seems never to have been born at all. He comes from afar, neither old nor young, always in the prime of life, master of all trades, full of guile, tainted with guilt yet boldly outfacing his accusers: Spirit? Yes, but, as fallen Adam, somewhat under-proof, and vaguely conscious that in spite of the great works he points to in his justification, he is still 'ultimendly respunchable for the hubbub caused in Edenborough'.

Anna Livia's death monologue is a long record of memories. Just before all utterance is stopped, before soul and body part company, she speaks a word that seems to me to express the final hope of the body that she is: 'mememormee'.

This word I interpret in the first place as 'memory'; and memory is a function of the mind which Joyce equated with imagination. It certainly plays its part in the operations of sympathy and empathy which are part of the equipment of every sensitive human being and forms a solid runway for the lapwing flights of the poet. And may it not also be taken as a bridge between the body and its appetites and functions and the soul with its aspirations? Anna Livia demands of memory not only that it shall summon up remembrance of things past, but also that it shall in some transcendent fashion restore to her the life she is losing.

This is made clear if we see the word also as 'Me, me, Ocean. Me.' This I take to be her final prayer that out of the welter of undifferentiated matter into which she is being dissolved, her very own body, her individual self, may be preserved and restored to her to live again as she lived before. It is her prayer for the resurrection of the body, but the life everlasting she desires is the life on earth she knew.

And so from 'the' full circle to 'riverrun'. World without end? Hardly. Joyce was much too wary an artist to allow any cosmological speculation to cramp the freedom of his factification. Besides, there are hints of ends (Judgment Day, Ragnarok) all through the book.

But now, at the end of my thread (and tether!) I ask myself how do the other elements fit into this central pattern to which I am committed? In particular Shem and Shaun. Evidently the twins live in another time-field. They are a recurrent pattern in human life, but their days are numbered. Joyce once told me that each of them had a child of his sister—perhaps in the Land of Nod. If the event is recorded in *Finnegans Wake* I have not yet discovered it. However, procreation does not of necessity confer fatherhood on the procreator, and, as I see it, Haveth Childers Everywhere does not devise that mystical estate upon his sons. Nor do they succeed him. That which does not suffer death has no need of a successor. That leaves them as symbols of the hungry generations for ever treading each other down.

'Who were Shem and Shaun the living sons or daughters of?'

Frederick J Hoffman

'THE SEIM ANEW': FLUX AND FAMILY IN
FINNEGANS WAKE

It is scarcely an original thought, but surely one worth repeating: Joyce began his career hating and fearful of flux, chaos, and disorder; he ended it, in *Finnegans Wake*, by making a virtue of the reality of flux. The sensual world is ever-present in his work. Colors symbolically and imagistically dominate within it; tastes, sounds, tactile sensations provide the vibrancy of the Dublin scene and of the world abroad, always in the act of 'doublin their mumper' (*Finnegans Wake*, p. 3). Beyond these matters, there is the autobiographical reference, which is more difficult to measure. There are several significant facts it will be useful to remember. Joyce's father is the 'pivot' of his reflections upon family; in the beginning, he is shocked by the disorder (and its attendant filth and stinks) that his father can cause simply by not being a responsible family man. Later, his father's aberrant ways, while still recalled, are less important than his charm, his good voice, and his love of the 'good time'. In the end, in *Finnegans Wake* the father principle, and the father who exemplifies it, undergoes a curious change; Joyce, the son of his father, becomes through his role as creator, the father of the father image who suffers and himself creates. As he puts it in *Finnegans Wake*: 'Creator he has created for his creatured ones a creation' (p. 29).

The story is perhaps a familiar one, and yet there are new insights into the family pattern. One of the major crises in modern literature (and, by implication, in modern society) concerns the stability of family. The great Jewish thinkers insist upon family cohesiveness; Catholics all but make a law of the inseparableness of man, wife and children. In the Protestant world, the individual responsibility overcomes family demands, and there occurs a breakdown of the idea of family as moral center. Max Weber and Carl Gustav Jung provide the economic and psychological versions of the decline.

The obvious truth is that the family is a microcosm of orders beyond it, geographical, cultural and universal. And, of course, the father becomes a 'major man', a creator and a primary cause at one and the same time. His acts, and the will behind them, are defined immediately and extensively in terms of their consequences. The disorder following upon the Joyce family's moves from one place to another, and upon the behavior of Joyce's father, is responsible for a crucial puzzle in Joyce's work. In the beginning, the creature tries to define himself simply by separating from the family and its religious supports. Joyce's attention is fixed upon the young creature who will rebel against his creator (both father and God, who are often interestingly merged in *Finnegans Wake*) by changing his status from that of creature to that of creator. Except in *Stephen Hero*, which we should really not consider as being in the 'Joyce canon' because he himself did not so consider it, Joyce consistently poses father against son or sons, measures the spatial and psychological distances between them, and muses over the puzzle and (at times) the farce of creation itself.

I believe that one of the great contributions made by *Finnegans Wake* to modern literary thought is its suggestion concerning a solution of the problems of father-family and creator-creature relationship. This is a solution worked out without benefit of either clergy or psychiatrist. Joyce's sources are characteristically 'modern', in the fact that they are varied, even esoteric, and the result of intellectual improvisation in the establishment of a 'tradition'.[1] The fact of most interest to us at this moment is not the cyclical theory of history, but the Viconian idea that God the creator, in the act of creation, commits 'original sin'.[2] To say the least, Vico's God is bemused in consequence of the act of creation; it is preceded by thunder (which is God's way of stammering and hence His admission of guilt). Earwicker plays the God role as the father-creator, but (as the creature of God) in the sense of Joyce's remark 'Teems of times and happy returns. The seim anew' (p. 215), he is also a part of a recurring process, which God had set going by His initial creative act.

II

It ought surely to be illuminating to consider some of the characteristic images according to which Joyce has tried to define the father and his relationship to family. To begin with, there is the characteristic to-do of 'building'. The 'seim anew' involves creation and re-creation and rebuilding from ruins. Fathers topple, but they also create in the sense of fashioning, building, designing. So the Finnegan of folklore is a hod-carrier who, having tippled, loses his balance and topples from his ladder, which in itself rests against a structure in the act of being 'built'. But before this happens, he has been 'Bygmester Finnegan, of the Stuttering Hand', this man 'of hod, cement and edifices' who 'piled buildung supra buildung pon the banks for the livers by the Soangso' (*Finnegans Wake*, p. 4). Of course there is no doubt of the sexual implications; the physical image of the god Finnegan-Earwicker-*et al.* is that of the body beginning with the rock at Howth and extending to Phoenix Park, with the monolith 'erection' of the Wellington (Wellingdone, Willingdone, etc.) monument 'standing' in the phallic role. A *structure* honors a great builder (and destroyer), but it is also the phallic instrument of the business of building. 'Buildung' has several other meanings: *bildung*, as in the *bildungsroman* which recounts human development; and *dung*, which here signifies the state of decay to which the body and the substance which supports its life returns. After all, it is from a dungheap that the letter defending HCE is accidentally recovered.

We need to appreciate the 'grand mixture' here: building (creating, fathering) is closely identified with the counter-activity of destroying and dying. The basic source of the Viconian cycle is the steady move of man and society from beginnings to endings to renewals. Earwicker 'dies a little' with each addition to his family; but he also literally *cohabits*, lies next to and on Anna Livia. The Liffey *flows* at his side and provides a continuing source of amniotic anticipation of life. It, and she, also flows into the seas, and thus is also dying; but in the course of moving out of life, she also moves back into it, the amniosis serving her as well as her children. The image of Earwicker's creativity is monolithic (his image is of rock and monumental structures); the key quality of Anna's is 'plurability'. Her resource is that of starting life, protecting it, and releasing it. Nothing so brilliantly defines this fusion of death and life as the closing-opening sentence of the *Wake*: 'A way a lone a last a loved a long the riverrun, past Eve and Adam's, from swerve of shore to bend of bay, brings us by a commodius vicus of recirculation back to Howth Castle and Environs' (pp. 628, 3). Moving out into the sea of death, Anna Livia, 'a lone', becomes daughterwife to his sonhusband; the life process goes on, and she is 'allaniuvia pulchrabelled' because 'Now a younger's there' (p. 627).

III

These acts of building, 'erecting', destroying, decaying, and renewing are more important in the perspective of Joyce's early creations. In a sense *Stephen Hero was* Joyce annotating his daily existence, and enhancing it; it is a diary of things happening and to come. Next, over a period of some eight years, Joyce replaced this manuscript with a 'portrait'.[3] The word is itself important: Stephen is no longer 'heroic', but the subject of a work done by a man who looks at him from a distance. The distance is not great, but it is fairly important: not only years, but the act of exile have determined it. Joyce, in leaving Dublin, separated himself from the self who lived there. The consequences are partly viewed in the irony and skeptical reserve with which he views his creature. He has not yet reached the stage of the Viconian God's puzzlement over the results of his creative act; but the Stephen of *Portrait* is a model exercise in the drama of youthful separation from authority; more, it is a way of defining the arrogation of authority, removing it from the world of teachers, priests, fathers, and investing it in the rebellious self.

The squalor of Stephen's home life is a consequence of the father's decline. The breaking of the home forces Stephen into the streets, away from the family center, and he observes there poverty, filth, chaos. 'He wanted to meet in the real world the unsubstantial image which his soul so constantly beheld' (*Portrait*, p. 65 [66]). His mind and senses entertain the prospects of sensual bliss, but he is wary of actual contact. On a trip to Cork with his father, he visits Queen's College; there, in the anatomy theatre, Stephen reads the word *Fœtus* 'cut several times in the dark stained wood' (p. 89 [92]). The word startles him into thinking about past students, who have ironically left, as a 'symbol of permanence', this sign of their interest for others to see.

Stephen associates the biological implications of the word with the chaotic world his father's indulgences have created. Biology abases the intellect, as Stephen believes, inferring from the 'den of monstrous images' he has himself tolerated and encouraged. Disappointment in the father causes him to seek other sources of authority. The Church is revived in his mind as a father substitute: the priest will be father, and he may himself be priest, which is to say, 'father', without the implications the word has in his own family. The Church acts temporarily in the role of providing order and protecting him from the chaos of the outside world. But ultimately it will have an opposite effect: infinite extensions of both bodily pain and the pain of absence haunt Stephen in the days of the retreat sermons. To become a priest, after having made full confession, occurs to him as a way through.

The important point in Stephen's education is not his temporary sense of vocation, but his eventual act of secular conversion. This conversion is partway a recovery of his appreciation of sensual beauty: 'Heavenly God! cried Stephen's soul, in an outburst of profane joy' (p. 171 [176]).[4] It is also an attempt to set 'beauty' against chaos: Stephen walks through the disorder of Dublin, shaking from his ears the sound of 'a mad nun screeching' (p. 175 [179]), trying to replace it with the songs of Ben Jonson or the 'dainty songs of the Elizabethans' (p. 176 [180]).

All of this is informed with an irony cultivated by Stephen's creator over a period of eight years of separation of creator from creature. The tone is sympathetic; he will 'hear him out'; and the discourses on beauty and creation are marvels in themselves. Like the library 'lecture' on Shakespeare's *Hamlet*, Stephen's discussion of *integritas*, *consonantia*, and *claritas* have the marks of genius but are nevertheless also locally and temporally caused. As before, he is trying to shut out the disorder caused by his father's defection. The 'many', the 'schwärmerei' of unordered life, is simply ugly and hateful, and needs to be kept within aesthetic bounds. Hence Stephen's mind works in terms of 'bounding lines', of precise forms and central illuminations. The great attractiveness of the 'epiphany' to him is not its divinity but its having marvellously worked in terms of a point of essence. In this way commonplace and even ugly moments may be invested with aesthetic power, in the sense that the 'ostensoir' of Baudelaire's 'Harmonie du soir' gives an aesthetic more than a religious illumination.

In all cases there is some one who assumes the role of the 'monothoid', the man who wishes to conquer the many by assuming it under the rubric of the one. Joyce's own conscience will not permit this easy way out of disorder; so the advocate of the one is not infrequently mocked, even–in the figure of a Lucifer, who arrogates God's power unto himself–treated as blasphemer. Stephen's career in *Ulysses* shows a further distance of created from creature. Here the riot of conundrum and paradox becomes even more outrageously amusing: two creators, who are two fathers (the one of the other, the other of himself); a father-god image who, having lost a son, seeks another and becomes not only father but God-companion to Stephen. Stephen's assertion of mind's power over thing is here even less convincing, because he is himself a victim of sensations which cannot be expelled as they were in the *Portrait*.

Ulysses is above all a testimony of the triumph of gestation over death. The 'Hades' episode reminds us clearly of the naturalistic odors and images of corruption; the 'conqueror worm' is treated as a comic inversion of its original function of horror. But the oncoming recurrences of life, as they do in *Finnegans Wake*, take the sting from the haunts of death (Bloom in the cemetery, Stephen staring in fright at the image of his dead mother who has risen to haunt him). As in *Finnegans Wake*, the father becomes the 'maker', the builder, whose 'erections' are solid achievements:

'. . . By heaven, Theodore Purefoy, thou hast done a doughty deed and no botch! Thou art, I vow, the remarkablest progenitor barring none in this chaffering allincluding most farraginous chronicle. Astounding! In her lay a Godframed Godgiven preformed possibility which thou hast fructified with thy modicum of man's work . . .' (*Ulysses*, p. 423 [554]).

In other words, the multiplicity of Dublin (the 'doublin their mumper' of *Finnegans Wake*) is no longer a frightful thing. The promise of Mrs Purefoy's ninth child, celebrated as it is in the 'farraginous chronicle' of 'Oxen of the Sun', has a significance beyond its adding to 'their mumper'.

IV

Finnegans Wake is the culminating act in Joyce's conquest of his fear of the many. Not only are Shem's 'heroic acts' mocked (exile, the writings, the search for an aesthetic surrogate for life); all attempts to secure him against the flux are ignominiously defeated. Momentarily a Lucifer in *Ulysses* (in a scene which has at least a 'drunken glory'), Shem becomes a comic devil in *Finnegans Wake*; and his rebellion against not only father and family but life itself is treated with rich irony. Shem is no longer a lonely and arrogant spirit, proudly announcing his *non serviam*; he is actually (in being Shaun's twin, hence his 'identical opposite') the reverse of himself. I think one may say that *Finnegans Wake* is an immense 'accommodation' of the many, and that the multiplicity of life is given order as an intrinsic quality of renewal and recurrence.

The 'seim anew', the father is no longer a disrespected, irresponsible creator; like Lawrence, Joyce atoned for early unflattering portraits by establishing and defending a 'father principle' in his late work. The designs of explanation in *Finnegans Wake* are no longer confined to the neat indulgences of mind's-play; they have been based upon principles of organic growth and decay, recurrence, opposites which combine to make identities, a universal set of fluctuant geometries, with the minds of the participants playfully enacting the role of comically erudite annotator upon the facts of existence.

I do not mean that the father is glorified; and he is certainly not elevated to the level to which Lawrence brings his memory of the father image. Joyce's HCE is not so much a god figure as he is the representative 'maker' of vital abundance and disorder, the 'folksforefather' (*Finnegans Wake*, p. 33). There is a constant stir and susurrus, which rises to loud clamor and subsides to 'confidential' gossip, but continues to surround his character. In other words, the 'truth' is as difficult to discover in *words* (each man uses words differently) as it is in things. Throughout, HCE is successor to Simon Dedalus, whose identity is public, associated with the children he has fathered, the friends he has made, the tavern, street, and out-of-doors comment and gossip he has stimulated and abetted. At the same time, HCE, like Bloom, is the alternate father figure as well: the foreigner, suspected of vague and shadowy sins, an intruder and invader. Joyce, the exile, makes his major figures exiles-in-Dublin, by way of compensation for his being Dubliner-in-Paris. The father of the *Wake* is therefore at the center of rumor, gossip, debate, and abuse; but he is solidly *there*, 'the pftjschute of Finnegan, erse solid man . . .' (p. 3).

One way of interpreting the prevailing confusion in the *Wake* is to suggest that it is an indispensable part of being itself; the Joycean conception of life is, as we know from *Ulysses*, that it is a turmoil, a riot of opposites defying and at the same time seeking identities. In Joyce's notebooks, the data of life are patches and fragments of language, phrase, color, and sound. Each portmanteau word or phrase can be counted upon to multiply several-fold the suggestion and sound of meaning. That this brouhaha is dramatized in terms of family disputes is understandable; it is in the family that humanity 'settles', as water slows and moves toward the calm center of a pool. This is, at least, the view of it in *Finnegans Wake*; the family quarrels in *Dubliners* and *Portrait* testify to the fact that Joyce's acceptance of the family as center comes late in his life, and is defined in an entirely different intellectual atmosphere from the Catholic Dublin father-priest authority suggested to him at the beginning.

It is not so much that Joyce has simply 'got over' his rebellion, but rather that the distance from his creatures which maturity put at his disposal helped him immeasurably in assessing the actual depth and value of the noise and vibration of human *ambiance*. Identity is no longer what it was in the *Portrait*: there it meant what one *separately was*. In the *Wake* it emerges from a 'welter' that is caused partly by contemporary circumstances, partly by the everpresence, immanence, *or* imminence, of recurrent identities. Or, as Joyce says in the *Wake*, 'by the coincidance of their contraries reamalgamerge in that indentity of undiscernibles' (pp. 49-50). The mixture is not only of gossip, rumor, and truth; it is also of good and evil. 'First we feel. Then we fall', Anna Livia says (p. 627). The 'fall' is indispensable to being; guilt is indicated in HCE's stammering, which is matched in the recurrence, ten times, of the thunder, or God's stammering. But the awareness of guilt is not in itself a fact of paralysing effect or of stunning importance. HCE 'emerges' or rises from his fall; each time, he creates as he sins, or sins as he creates. Human fertility does eventually impress identity upon the world of relations; the identity which 'reamalgamerges' transcends the confusion of human strife over names, libels, lies, and similar calumnies. The ultimate aim is to provoke recognition of (1) the 'I' (the 'mishe mishe' of the *Wake*'s beginning), and (2) the family, which is a cluster of polarities and identities.

The family polarities rest chiefly with the twin sons. Shem is the great abstracter, the man who wants to push outward, in cyclical speculation, to put reality into the garments of semblance, in 'the weirdest of all pensible ways' (p. 152). Further, he is the Dubliner in exile on the Continent, as his father is the 'invader exile' in Dublin. There is no doubt that section seven of part one is 'editorial', an echo of Joyce's critics, but at the same time an expression of Joyce's ultimate separation from the Stephen of *Portrait* and *Ulysses*. The passages are now familiar enough to the readers of the *Wake*: '... Tumult, son of Thunder, self exiled in upon his ego, a nightlong a shaking betwixtween white or reddr hawrors, noonday-terrorised to skin and bone by an ineluctable phantom (may the Shaper have mercery on him!) writing the mystery of himsel in furniture' (p. 184). The *doubles entendres* are sufficiently obvious: himself, but also him plus cell (which goes with 'self exiled in upon his ego'); furniture means things, patches and fragments fitted together in a design which is a mystery to all but himself. But he is also a 'premature gravedigger, seeker of the nest of evil in the bosom of a good word' (p. 189), a scavenger among ashes and dung, a connoisseur of obscenity and obscurity, 'shemming amid everyone's repressed laughter to conceal your scatchophily by mating, like a thoroughpaste prosodite, masculine monosyllables of the same numerical mus' (p. 190).

That this characterization of Shem elides skillfully into the section devoted to Anna Livia Plurabelle is important enough. In the role of Mercius (the polar opposite of Justius), Shem appeals to his mother ('. . . I who oathily forswore the womb that bore you and the paps I sometimes sucked . . .', p. 193); and the sound of contentiousness becomes a punning mixture of the 'quoi?' for 'what', and a quacking sound, identical with the sound that Lucky makes in Beckett's *Waiting for Godot*. For Anna Livia, the sounds are resumed once again as gossip, but (in the tone of rivers, forever renewing themselves in their 'riverrun') also as a 'bildung' story, the move from the 'young thin pale soft shy slim slip of a thing' to the mother and the progenitress of the 'seim anew': 'Anna was, Livia is, Plurabelle's to be' (p. 215).

In the end, the noise has abated, the lessons and lesions have been given, and we come back to the facts of gestation, of biological renewal, of the great erection and the smooth amniotic flow. As the great Theodore Purefoy is praised for his 'doughty deed' in *Ulysses*, so HCE merits the distinction of 'Haveth Childers Everywhere'. In the Mime of Mick, Nick and the Maggies, the game is to find '. . . what is that which is one going to prehend?' Or, 'The howtosayto itiswhatis hemustwhomust worden schall' (p. 223). Shem (in the role of Glugg) finds the teeming world 'Truly deplurabel!' (p. 224). But the 'coincidance' continues around poor Glugg, defying his effort to make one stand where once were many: the dance of cycles and generations, through 'Endles of Eons efter Dies of Eirae doeslike' (pp. 226–7); in other words, the 'seim anew' and many 'happy returns'. The 'essies' are 'impures' (p. 234), as they are in the world of Beckett's creatures.[5] The ascent of man becomes the 'assent of man' (p. 252), and ultimately human reality is accepted as an ever-changing, always certain merging of 'essies' and 'possies'.

In *Finnegans Wake*, Joyce put the crown upon his celebration of the 'acceptance world', which in *Ulysses* had been featured in the mind of his street-roaming, musing exile, Bloom. Stephen saw the disorder and filth of life too, and even sought a fusion of space and time (the *nacheinander* and the *nebeneinander* of 'Proteus'); but his struggle against corruption and death becomes less and less an heroic and lonely stand against his 'duvlin sulph', and yields to the very teeming profusion of life that is graphically given in *Ulysses*, more complexly offered in the *Wake*. For not only is the Stephen figure of the *Wake* given with less respect; he moves into and out of his twin self, so that their polarities become identities. Evidences of resemblance, 'The seim anew' triumph over disparities. The father who earlier had merited the scorn of his rebellious son is now respected *and* opposed, fought *and* joined, because the principles of diffusion and twinness must eventually prove out as variations within a dominating and recurring identity.

NOTES

1 The obvious book to read in this connection is James S. Atherton's *The Books at the Wake* (New York, Viking, 1960). Joyce is 'characteristically modern' in the sense that Pound and Eliot are – not necessarily in conclusions reached but in the intellectual machinery used in getting to them
2 See Atherton, p. 31
3 In September 1907 Joyce announced to his brother Stanislaus plans to revise *Stephen Hero* thoroughly. This was the beginning of *Portrait*, the last pages of which Joyce sent off in November 1914 for publication in *The Egoist*.
4 'Her image had passed into his soul for ever and no word had broken the holy silence of his ecstasy' (p. 172 [176])
5 See Lucky's 'Think piece' in *Waiting for Godot* (New York, Evergreen Books, 1954, pp. 28–9)

Vivian Mercier

JAMES JOYCE AND THE MACARONIC TRADITION

'Cranly was speaking (as was his custom when he walked with other gentlemen of leisure) in a language the base of which was Latin and the superstructure of which was composed of Irish, French and German . . .' (*Stephen Hero*, 106 [92]).

'It is told in sounds in utter that, in signs so adds to, in universal, in polygluttural, in each auxiliary neutral idiom, sordomutics, florilingua, sheltafocal, flayflutter, a con's cubane, a pro's tutute, strassarab, ereperse and anythongue athall' (*Finnegans Wake*, 117).

'Boildoyle and rawhoney on me when I can beuraly forsstand a weird from sturk to finnic in such a patwhat as your rutterdamrotter. Onheard of and umscene!' (*FW*, 17).

Joyce's letters, as well as the first passage from the *Wake* quoted above (in which *sheltafocal* means 'word of shelta'), show that he knew something of shelta, a tinkers' jargon which mingles Gaelic and English elements in distorted form: 'I fancy it is some corrupt Irish written backwards and used by gentlemen who don't pay the rent' (*Letters*, 256). One wonders if he read R. A. S. Macalister's *The Secret Languages of Ireland*, first published in 1937.[1] It contains a great deal of lively information about shelta and about many other manifestations of the traditional Irish love for erudite, obscure, and —above all—polyglot writing and speech. More entertaining still is a long passage[2] in which Macalister compared what he had seen of *Work in Progress* with the *Hisperica Famina*—that curious example of fifth- or sixth-century Latinity which borrows words from Greek and Hebrew yet refers to the speech of the surrounding populace as '*scottigenum . . . eulogium*', meaning presumably the Gaelic language of Ireland.[3] E. K. Rand had in fact made the same comparison as early as 1931.[4]

Even if Joyce was only dimly aware of the Irish polyglot tradition, we can safely claim that the principle of macaronic writing was known to him in his undergraduate days or very soon after. When Cranly remarks in *Stephen Hero*, '*Nos ad manum ballum jocabimus*' (We'll play at handball), or Stephen says of Cranly's hat, '*Sicut bucketus est*' (It's like a bucket), their language is macaronic in the strictest sense of the word: they are giving Latin terminations to purely vernacular words like 'bucket' and 'ball'.

Octave Delepierre, in his comprehensive book *Macaronéana*, reserves the term *Macaronic* for those literary dialects in which 'the writer . . . takes his roots from his mother tongue and adds Latin termination and inflection'.[5] He goes on to distinguish several other related techniques. *Hybrid* mingles two or more languages without assimilating their inflection to Latin, as when Cranly says, '*Feuc[h] an eis super stradam . . .*' (Look at the ice on the street). The editors of the Irish *Liber Hymnorum* and the German monk Notker Balbulus write like this almost without conscious effort; Thomas Mann tried to imitate the latter in *The Holy Sinner*.[6] *Bog Latin* or *Kitchen Latin* (*latin de cuisine*) 'consists in the literal translation into Latin of phrases from the mother tongue'.[7] The best example of this from Joyce's early work occurs in *A Portrait of the Artist*: '*Ego credo ut vita pauperum est simpliciter atrox, simpliciter sanguinarius atrox, in Liverpoolio*' (216 [220]). This translates directly as, 'I believe that the life of the poor is simply awful, simply bloody awful, in Liverpool', but it would give Cicero the horrors, supposing he were able to make sense of it at all. Finally, *Pedantesque* 'makes the Latin word take on the forms of the vulgar tongue'.[8] The classic example occurs in Book II, chapter 6, of Rabelais, where Pantagruel meets the Limousin who is returning home, '*De l'alme, inclyte, et celebre academie que l'on vocite Lutece*.'[9] Pedantesque occurs pretty much *passim* in *Finnegans Wake*: 'A spathe of calyptrous glume involucrumines the perinanthean Amenta: fungoalgaceous muscafilicial graminopalmular planteon . . .' (p. 613).

If I were asked to define the language of the *Wake* in Delepierre's terms, I should call it Hybrido-Pedantesque, since words from a great many languages besides Latin, 'from sturk to finnic', take on English inflection. (I assume that the basic language of the *Wake* is English and should be pronounced as such, except for certain prose passages printed in italics.) Of strict Macaronic I cannot find any examples more than a word or two long, such as *aqua in buccat* (p. 296.30) – which makes no sense *as Latin*.

Joyce is most original, to my mind, in his all-pervading use of the polyglot pun, but even this is not something entirely new. For instance, Teofilo Folengo, the Old Master of Macaronic, speaks of '*Pancificae . . . Musae*', his 'paunchmaking Muses', with an obvious play on *pacificae* (peacemaking, peaceful).[10] While Joyce may not have known Folengo's work, he did know that of Francis Mahony, 'Father Prout', who was once a master at Clongowes Wood College, Joyce's first prep. school. Here is a typical O'Mahony pun, combining Greek and English, from 'A Plea for Pilgrimages':

'The Athenians thought that the ghosts of departed heroes were transferred to our fortunate island, which they call, in the war song of Harmodius and Aristogiton, the land of O's and Macs:

Φιλταθ' 'Αρμοδι, ουτε που τεθνηκας,
Νησοις δ'εν ΜΑΚ αρ' ΩΝ σε φασιν ειναι.'[11]

Joyce's habit of mind was intensely traditional—never more so than when it seemed superficially most revolutionary. Cranly noted the same trait in Stephen: '—It is a curious thing, do you know, . . . how your mind is supersaturated with the religion in which you say you disbelieve' (*Portrait*, 240 [244]).

Perhaps I have offered sufficient proof that at the verbal level *Finnegans Wake* belongs to a definite tradition, one in which Joyce was consciously working. I even dream that I have found a quotation from the *Wake* which clinches matters—as if anything so volatile as the meaning of a passage in that work could serve as a clinching tool: '. . . the memories of the past and the hicnuncs of the present embellishing the musics of the futures from Miccheruni's band . . .' (*FW*, 407). I admit that 'Miccheruni's band' means primarily 'Marconi's wave-band', for the entire passage deals with a broadcast by Shaun and contains the word 'marconimasts'. Furthermore, since Marconi was Italian, a reference to *maccheroni* seems almost inevitable. ('Micky Rooney's band' appears in *Ulysses*, 'Sirens' episode, p. 289 [373].) Still, the passage I have quoted *can* bear on one level the following interpretation: 'Memories of the past and hiccups from the here-and-now of the present embellishing with belches the literature of the future through a macaronic style which binds them together.'

Actually, Joyce's affinity with the macaronic tradition is more striking at the archetypal level than at the verbal one. The word *macharonea* was first used by Tifi Odasi of Padua about 1490 to describe a satiric poem written in what I have already called strict Macaronic.¹² A high percentage of the Italian or Paduan dialect words contained in it are obscene. Folengo later exalted this practice into a principle, saying, 'the coarser the words are, the greater the macaronic elegance they supply'.¹³ I cannot decide whether the macaronic poets thought that an overall Latin coloring palliated the vernacular obscenities or, on the contrary, enhanced them. Nor can I decide which is more obscene, *Finnegans Wake*, which never uses *le mot cru*, or *Ulysses*, which always does.

I am stressing obscenity – not pornography, remember – because as I see it, the archetype of macaronic poetry is some form of saturnalia – a ritual celebrating a father-god who is also a giant.¹⁴ He is a benevolent yet dangerous all-father, who, like Saturn, can swallow his sons as well as beget them. He has a bride as monstrous as himself. The ordinary men and women who are satirized in the early Paduan macaronics bulk huge as giants when the poets begin to describe their sexual characteristics. Here is a male figure – an unmistakably male figure – from the anonymous *Nobile Vigonce Opus*:

Inflatus largo perdet sub pectore venter
Et petenecchium densissima silva videtur
Est subter brutus tanquam de porco buellus
Cum coionacis pendens tiransque chaçochius
*Qui semper vellet largas intrare potifas . . .*¹⁵

His swollen belly and other imposing organs make him a fit gargantuan mate for this female from the *Macharonea* of Odasi:

Inque sinu patent gemine de pelle tetaze
Quarumque minor esse[?] poterit tocare bilickum . . .
In mediis gambis apud foramina culi . . .
Ingens apparet variisque meatibus antrum . . .
Nomine quo proprio vocatur ubique potaza . . .
Illic cum velis possent natare galiae . . . ¹⁶

While the description of her breasts, hanging to the navel or below, seems like mere comic exuberance, the 'cavern' in which 'galleys could float with all sail set' sets one thinking of river-goddesses – not merely Anna Livia, but others from Celtic mythology, of whom I shall say more in a moment.

Teofilo Folengo, though he directly influenced Rabelais and, as we have seen, justified macaronic obscenity, seems chaste beside his predecessors; however, unlike them, he quite explicitly writes about giants. Baldus, who gives his name to Folengo's *magnum opus*, a macaronic epic or romance in twenty-five books, is five fathoms tall, but still only one-eighth the height of his comrade Fracassus.[17]

Perhaps the ultimate literary ancestor of all macaronic and polyglot giants is the legendary Bishop Golias, patron saint of the *goliardi*, who in turn must be a reincarnation of the biblical Goliath and thus a 'type' of Antichrist. I do not know of any Golias poems in strict Macaronic, but there are some in Hybrid.[18] As for the giant Gargantua, he derived from folklore as well as literature, for Rabelais's immediate source was a chap-book.[19] Henri Gaidoz, the eminent Celtic scholar, even claimed a mythological origin for him in *Gargantua: essai de mythologie celtique* (Paris, 1868). I have not been able to obtain this book, but here are some excerpts from a review of it:

'M. Gaidoz believes that the giant Gargantua was originally a Celtic god ... a god who appeared in the Gallo-Roman inscriptions under the name of Hercules, but whose true name was lost, while his epithet *Gargant*, "the devourer", was preserved; and this epithet had for origin the human sacrifices which were offered him. "I learn from M. Fr Lenormant", he says, "that at Rouen on the feast-day of St Romain (October 23), little figures two or three centimeters high used to be sold; these represented grotesque men furnished with the emblem of Priapus. These figures were called *Gargans*; and the unmarried girls bought them and put them in their bodices in the hope of finding a husband more easily...."' [20]

It is very tempting to identify this nameless Gaulish god with the Irish god known as the Dagda (literally *dag-dia*, 'good god'), or as Eochaid Ollathair, Eochaid the All-Father. In the words of the late Marie-Louise Sjoestedt: '... the Dagda is good at everything. He is not only first among magicians; he is a formidable fighter.... His superiority rests in this omnipotence which derives from his omniscience. And his omniscience is expressed in another of his titles, *Ruad Ro-fhessa* ("Lord of Perfect Knowledge")....' [21]

As Mlle Sjoestedt continues, this awesome god suddenly begins to look oddly like HCE or the comic Finn mac Cumaill of Irish folklore:

'The figure of the chieftain-father bears the stamp of a primitive style which redactors have deliberately pressed to a grotesque extreme. Hideous and pot-bellied, he wears a cowl and short tunic like that of the Gaulish god of the mallet; but in Irish sagas long garments are a measure of the dignity of the wearer, and this tunic is the ordinary attire of churls. . . . The enormous club, mounted on wheels, which he drags along, is so heavy that eight men would be required to carry it. . . . With one end of the club he can kill nine men; with the other he restores them to life. Lord of life and death by means of this magic club, he is also lord of abundance by means of his inexhaustible cauldron, from which "no one goes away without being satisfied".'[22]

The club reminds us of Hercules, with whom Gargantua's supposed Celtic prototype was identified. It also reminds us of Shaun's deathbone and Shem's lifewand. As for the 'cauldron of plenty', it is everywhere implicit in Folengo and Rabelais. Folengo's macaronic Muses live in a sort of Schlaraffenland or Land of Cockaigne, amid a landscape composed chiefly of *macaroni*-or rather of what we should now call *gnocchi*. An Italian scholar, Luigi Messedaglia, has written a work of over two hundred pages which deals almost exclusively with the vinicultural, agricultural, horticultural and culinary information crammed into the *Baldus* by Folengo.[23] How much eating there is in *Finnegans Wake* I would find it hard to estimate, but there is certainly a gargantuan amount of it, as well as of drinking.

As we might expect, the Dagda himself is a great feaster–and a great lover. His enemies the Fomorians make him eat a giant meal under pain of death, but he gobbles it up easily and appears to be still hungry: 'After the feast the Dagda has intercourse with his enemy's daughter, not without difficulty for his stomach is greatly distended. . . . While the redactors delighted in emphasizing the grotesque obscenity of this double episode, one can recognize it as a ritual manifestation of the powers of voracity and sexual vigour which are attributes necessary to the prestige of a barbarous chieftain.'[24]

The union of chieftain-father-god with river-mother-goddess, so fundamental to *Finnegans Wake*, occurs at least twice in the mythology of the Dagda. He meets the *Morrígan* by a river: '. . . in the act of washing, "with one foot south of the water and one foot north of the water". . . . They have intercourse, and the place is called "The Bed of the Couple" ever since.'[25] Again, Oengus-the 'Angus Dagdasson' of *FW*, 248–is begotten by the Dagda upon Boann, the River Boyne, in a night that lasts nine months. In the words of *Finnegans Wake*: 'I abridged with domfine norsemanship till I had done abate her maidan race, my baresark bride . . .' (*FW*, 547). Here HCE is not only describing his wedding night with ALP, but also telling how as the Scandinavian founder of Dublin he bridged the River Liffey and made it flow in a more confined channel. Mlle Sjoestedt's *Gods and Heroes of the Celts* was first published, in Paris, a year after the *Wake*. She finds in Celtic mythology what Joyce found in all mythology: '. . . a male principle of society to which is opposed a female principle of nature. . . .'[26]

The reader may wonder why I have laid such stress on the Dagda, whose name barely appears in the *Wake*, while I have neglected Finn mac Cumaill, type of all Irish giants, whose name occurs hundreds of times. My reason is that the Dagda indisputably represents a more primitive level of tradition, where the archetype can be seen more clearly. As a matter of fact, every history of Gaelic literature glibly relates how 'the folk mind' took over the legend of Finn from the aristocracy and 'debased' it. If Finn was originally a historical character – I personally do not believe he was – the Irish people chose an odd way of debasing him, for they gave him all the attributes of a god. I don't suppose there is a single motif in the myth of the Dagda that one could not parallel in the Finn cycle – if not in literature, then in folklore.

I hope I have now established to the reader's satisfaction a linkage between chieftain gods, folklore giants, and the heroes of polyglot literature – or at any rate the heroes of Folengo, Rabelais and Joyce. Joyce must have discovered the connection for himself by conscious reasoning, whereas the other two presumably hit by accident upon a group of folklore motifs which seemed to offer a suitable framework for humor, fantasy and satire.

But why should Hybrid or Macaronic be a peculiarly appropriate medium in which to narrate the deeds of giants or to record their speech? Northrop Frye offers a partial explanation:

'The gigantic figures in Rabelais, the awakened forms of the bound or sleeping giants that meet us in *Finnegans Wake* and the opening of *Gulliver's Travels*, are expressions of a creative exuberance of which the most typical and obvious sign is the verbal tempest, the tremendous outpouring of words in catalogues, abusive epithets and erudite technicalities which since the third chapter of Isaiah (a satire on female ornament) has been a feature, and almost a monopoly, of third-phase satire.'[27]

Here 'creative exuberance' is assigned as the principal cause for both the 'gigantic figures' and the 'verbal tempest'. But, as we have seen, it might be equally true to say that it is the giants who are responsible for the creative exuberance and hence also for the verbal tempest. Frye's suggestion is at best a half-truth.

To answer my own question I am almost tempted to postulate some kind of anti-Christian ritual involving the worship of Golias in a macaronic parody of Church Latin. Indeed, we know that the goliards were infamous for their parodies of the Mass, many of which, including a Gamblers' Mass and a Drunkards' Mass, survive in good imitations of ecclesiastical Latin.[28] If I knew of any such parody in Macaronic, especially one which exalted Golias, I should feel that my case was well on the way to being proved. Even if such a Mass were said only as a blasphemous joke, without any consciously Satanic overtones, it would in effect be an act of worship dedicated to the old gods.

However, all the above paragraph is highly speculative, whereas another type of mock ritual, one whose existence cannot be disputed, may have far greater relevance. In *The Golden Bough* Frazer comments on the similarity and probable identity—in spite of the disparity between their seasons—of the Roman saturnalia and the modern Italian carnival.[29] We may well ask if the earliest Italian macaronic poems were not written to celebrate—directly or indirectly—the king and queen of the carnival. Even today King Carnival is traditionally conceived of as a giant: his ghost haunts Macy's Thanksgiving Day parade. The *Nobile Vigonce Opus* already quoted could easily be performed as a series of set speeches delivered in turn by the poet and the gargantuan Vigonce (if that be the correct nominative form of his name). It so happens that Fossa's *Virgiliana*, a very early Macaronic poem, versifies the date of its composition— 2 March 1494.[30] Now, Shrove Tuesday 1495 fell on 3 March; therefore, if Fossa followed the then common practice of dating the year from 25 March, he completed his poem on the eve of carnival in 1495. No doubt such poems graced a sort of intra-mural university celebration of Mardi Gras.[32] Still, even at this distant remove the verses celebrated the Sacred Marriage of Saturn with Tellus—the father-god with the mother-goddess.

If these explanations seem too specific to bear out my theory of an underlying archetype, may I suggest just one more? One of the Dagda's titles was 'Lord of Perfect Knowledge'. Of Finn mac

Cumaill we read: '... whenever he put his thumb into his mouth and sang through *teinm laida* [a divinatory incantation], then whatever he had been ignorant of would be revealed to him.'[32] Perhaps the tremendous erudition of Rabelais and Joyce, the polished Virgilian hexameters of Folengo, were no more than appropriate to the celebration of so erudite a god.[33]

NOTES

1 R. A. Stewart Macalister, *The Secret Languages of Ireland* (Cambridge, 1937). It seems certain now that Joyce did read this book. See Adaline Glasheen's article in *A Wake Newslitter*, No. 10 (February 1963), pp. 1–3

2 Macalister, pp. 78–9

3 The best edition is F. J. H. Jenkinson, *The Hisperica Famina* (Cambridge, 1908)

4 E. K. Rand, 'The Irish flavor of Hisperica Famina', *Studien zur lateinischen Dichtung des Mittelalters*, ed. W. Stach and H. Walther (Dresden, 1931)

5 Octave Delepierre, *Macaronéana* (Paris, 1850), p. 14. My trans.

6 For Notker (whose Latin nickname means 'The Stammerer'), see Delepierre, p. 4. *The Irish Liber Hymnorum*, ed. J. H. Bernard and R. Atkinson, Henry Bradshaw Soc. XIII, XIV (London, 1898)

7 Delepierre, p. 9

8 *Ibid*, pp. 18–19

9 Pantagruel says to the Limousin, '*Tu escorches le latin.*' *Almus, inclytus*, and *vocito* are Latin words that have never become acceptable in French; *Lutetia*, the Latin name for Paris, has, however

10 Merlin Cocai (Teofilo Folengo), *Le Maccheronee*, ed. Alessandro Luzio (Bari, 1911), I, 47

11 Francis Mahony, *The Works of Father Prout*, ed. Charles Kent (London, 1881), p. 33. When not being punned on by Mahony, the Greek words mean roughly: 'Beloved Harmodius, you are not dead anywhere, but they say you are in the Islands of the Blest.' The last three words translate the suggestive Greek word *makarōn*. Oh blest macaronic!

12 See John Hodgkin, 'Bibliography of Tifi Odassis' [sic] Macharonea', *La Bibliofilia*, XXVI (Maggio-Giugno, 1924), 49–56

13 *Le Maccheronee*, ed. Luzio, II, 285: *quo magis grossiliora* [*vocabula*] *sunt eo magis macaronicam adducunt elegantiam* ...

14 Richard Ellmann, *James Joyce* (New York, 1959), p. 423, tells how Joyce often attended 'the fertility rite, *Sächselüte* (the ringing of six o'clock), a Zurich ceremony which celebrates the burial of winter'. The *Bögg* or winter demon, a male effigy about sixty feet high, is destroyed by fireworks and a bonfire in April each year

15 Octave Delepierre, *Macaronéana Andra* (London, 1862), p. 15. My tentative translation follows: 'His swollen belly hangs under his broad chest and his pubic hair seems to be a very thick wood. Below it is an ugly scrotum (?) like that of a

boar, weighed down with testicles, and a dragging penis which would always wish to enter wide vaginas.' This is not an adequate translation, since all the sexual terms are highly colloquial Italian words thinly disguised by Latin terminations

16 *Ibid*, pp. 80–1: 'And on her bosom twin breasts lie exposed, of which the smaller could touch her navel; . . . between her legs near the inlets of her buttocks . . . there appears a huge cavern with various passages . . ., which is called everywhere by its rightful name of *potaza* [cunt]; . . . galleys could float there with all sail set . . .'

17 *Histoire maccaronique de Merlin Coccaie*, ed. G. Brunet (Paris, 1859), pp. 60–1. In default of an English translation, this French one will prove helpful to those whose appetite for macaronics is not insatiable

18 See *Les Poésies des Goliards*, ed. and tr. Olga Dobiache-Rojdestvensky (Paris, 1931), pp. 114–15, 140

19 See, e.g., the Classiques Garnier *Œuvres de Rabelais*, ed. Louis Moland (Paris, n.d.), I, lx–lxi

20 *Revue celtique*, I (1870–2), 139. My trans. I have since read the essay by Gaidoz in *Revue archéologique*, nouvelle série, XVIII (septembre, 1868), 172–91, but the gist of it is faithfully given by the present quotation

21 Marie-Louise Sjoestedt, *Gods and Heroes of the Celts*, tr. Myles Dillon (London, 1949), p. 39

22 *Ibid*, pp. 39–40

23 Luigi Messedaglia, 'Aspetti della realtà storica in Merlin Cocai', *Atti del Reale Istituto Veneto di scienze, lettere ed arti*, Anno academico 1938–9, Tomo XCVIII, Parte II: Cl. di Scienze mor. e lett., pp. 33–263

24 Sjoestedt, p. 41

25 *Ibid*

26 *Ibid*, p. 93

27 Northrop Frye, *Anatomy of Criticism* (Princeton, 1957), p. 236

28 See, e.g., Octave Delepierre, *La Parodie* (London, 1870), pp. 34 ff.

29 James George Frazer, *The Golden Bough*, 1-vol. abridged ed. (New York, 1940), p. 586

30 Delepierre, *Macaronéana Andra*, p. 47

31 A remarkable survival of the saturnalia was to be found at the Universities of Oxford, Cambridge and Dublin until the eighteenth century: a 'lord of misrule' known suggestively as *Terrae Filius* ('The Son of the Earth') was chosen from among the students to deliver 'a satirical oration at the various public Acts of the University . . . poking fun or throwing dirt on students and those in authority alike.' Constantia Maxwell, *A History of Trinity College, Dublin, 1591–1892* (Dublin, 1946), p. 95. See also *ibid*, pp. 94, 96. The speeches, though not apparently ever in strict macaronic, employed both Latin and English, often obscenely. A standard work is Nicholas Amhurst, *Terrae Filius* (London, 1726)

32 *Ancient Irish Tales*, ed. Tom Peete Cross and Clark Harris Slover (New York, 1936), p. 365

33 Some of the material in this essay has been treated from a different viewpoint in Chapter 3, 'Macabre and Grotesque Humour in the Irish Tradition', of my book *The Irish Comic Tradition* (Oxford, 1962), pp. 47–77

Fritz Senn

INSECTS APPALLING

Finnegans Wake teems with insects. Its hero is an earwig; his family is introduced at the end of the first chapter as a verminous horde: 'he's such a grandfallar, with a pocked wife in pickle that's a flyfire and three lice nittle clinkers, two twilling bugs and one midgit pucelle' (29.6). Above all, the fable of the 'Ondt and the Gracehoper' is consistently entomological. Joyce's heavy emphasis on this particular crawl of life must have several reasons. One may be that insects bring to mind the irresistible fecundity and the ubiquitous persistence of low animal vitality; another that, by their metamorphoses through various stages, insects are ideally suited to stand for the important aspect of perpetual changing forms in the *Wake*. I believe that one further significance of the insect theme may warrant more attention than it has so far received. The Gracehoper in the fable intends 'to commence insects' (414.26): to commence, or beget, or breed, insects corresponds, it seems, to committing incest.

That Joyce is doing more than momentarily availing himself of an easy opportunity to permute a few letters may be borne out by the following considerations.

Incest looms large in *FW*, not, in the first place, because of Joyce's indebtedness to Freudian doctrine (though that plays its part) but simply because, in its own terms, everything takes place within the one family. Lovers ultimately are parents, while children, brothers and sisters, are all as 'entomate as intimate could pinchably be'. Appropriately, several groups of insects, notably ants and bees (where the burden of parturition is relegated to one female queen), are necessarily incestuous. Incest occurs also in many of the myths on which *FW* repeatedly draws: creative paternal gods and protoparents entail an incestuous origin of gods and men. This connexion may explain to some extent why the 'Ondt and the Gracehoper' contains an abundance of references to both insects and creator-gods, especially Egyptian ones, who were notoriously incestuous.

Incest need not be defined too narrowly. Etymologically (relying on 'his good smetterling of entymology', 417.4, we may deduce that some knowledge of etymology, in an entomological context, can yield intimations about human psychology, since in Greek the butterfly, Ger. *Schmetterling*, could symbolize the soul), incest is simply impurity or unchastity, Lat. *incestus* (*in-*, *castus*). Joyce drives this point home: 'even if only in chaste' (414.28). (It is possible that 'puce for shame', four lines later, hints at the German word *Blutschande*, blood-shame=incest. Puce suggests the colour of blood; all blushing is, come to think of it, shame expressed by the blood.)

If we prefer to take a standpoint different from that of the Viennese school and, along with Saint Thomas and Stephen Dedalus (*Ulysses*, p. 205 [264]), liken incest to 'an avarice of the emotions', we can easily point to avarice, emotional and material, in the character of the Ondt, finding this confirmed in 'andt's avarice' (268.11). But the Viennese school has, nevertheless, some relevant contributions to make. In the Freudian view (Joyce was aware that Freud's name means *joy* and this colours the Gracehoper's 'joyicity', 414.23), repressed desire for, and fear of, incest causes internal conflicts, and serious disturbances. Human nature may, of course, be seen as divided or torn between a high, spiritual, or divine part, and a low and bestial one. This splitting up is one more reason why insects and gods are lumped together in the 'Ondt and the Gracehoper'. One case in point is 'Bog' (416.19), containing the Slavonic word, *bog*, for 'god', and suggesting 'bug'. The same dichotomy shows in the very name of the Ondt, expressive of bourgeois morality: Ondt, as has often been pointed out, is Norwegian for evil, but, significantly, the adjective appears in its neuter form, referring therefore to an 'it' or, for our purposes, to the Id, while the name amounts, anagrammatically speaking, to the perennial prohibition of the Super-ego: 'Don't'.[1]

The same division into two parts is present, again etymologically, in the name 'insect': Lat. *in-sectum*, cut or split up. Insects moreover evoke, in general, repugnance and disgust–a reaction analogous to the aversion felt by some at thoughts of copulation, pregnancy and procreation. Puerile purity and stainlessness ('Stainusless', 237.11, and 'puerity', 237.25, occur near a cluster of allusions to the Egyptian *Book of the Dead*) may become supreme virtues:

woman may come to be regarded as unclean and contemptible. Compare the deprecating substitution of 'foods for vermin' (239.17) for 'votes for women', in a passage that is echoed in the fable of the 'Ondt and the Gracehoper' (415.19).[2] Freud comments: 'Small animals and vermin are substitutes for little children, e.g. undesired sisters or brothers. To be infected with vermin is often the equivalent for pregnancy.'[3] Note that the paragraph beginning at 239.16, which deals with the Annunciation, does not lack a touch of implied incest: the Virgin Mary, daughter of God, who conceives of the Holy Ghost and gives birth to Jesus, is daughter, wife, and mother of what is, after all, one divine person.

The relation of Stephen Dedalus, an early incarnation of the Gracehoper, with his mother can be, and has been, scrutinized with recourse to psychoanalytical terminology. Thus it may be worth noting that in *A Portrait* Stephen is beset with lice and has to be washed by his mother. Similarly, in *Ulysses*, her image has become associated with 'the blood of squashed lice from the children's shirts' (p. 10 [10]). In *Stephen Hero*, Stephen views Mother Church with symptomatically intense feelings of loathing and disgust: 'He seemed to see the vermin begotten in the catacombs. . . . Like the plague of locusts. . . . Contempt of [the body] human nature, weakness, nervous tremblings, fear of day and joy . . . beset the body burdened and disaffected in its members by its black tyrannous lice . . . every natural impulse . . . had been corroded by the pest of these vermin' (p. 194 [173]). In the 'Circe' episode old Virag and Bloom are voluble on the theme of insects, vermin, coition, sexology, and woman (pp. 515–17 [631–3]).

Thus it may not be surprising if honest Shaun, dimly conscious perhaps that his subject is going to be somewhat unpalatable, experiences some qualms when about to embark on his tale. That may be why he starts off with an apology and an attempt at a disguise ('apologuise', 414.16), and why he has first to negotiate a hundred-letter-long cough of embarrassment, occurring significantly after the consanguineous and insectuous word 'cousis': cousin and sis, but also French *cousin*, gnat. His audience did well to encourage him: 'Have mood!' (*Habe Mut*, Ger. for 'Take courage'). I suspect this is meant to lead us back to another injunction to muster up courage: 'Mummum' (259.10), *Mumm* being a colloquial German expression for courage. This word immediately introduces chapter ten, the geometry lesson, which is concerned with the sons' knowledge of their mother's genital organs—a tabooed subject ('Mum! Mum!') if ever there was one. It takes courage to tackle it, just as it takes courage to venture on the related fable of the disputing insects, in which, incidentally, 'Mummum' is echoed as 'Hummum' (416.2). The subject is identical, and the brothers' summum bone of contention is always their mum, or their sister.

Incest may be natural with gods, men, and insects, but ultimendly it is a crime and a sin. Thus it is not only one cause of the perpetual crimean wars of opposing sect-arian fathers and sons and brothers, but it is also intimately involved in Earwicker-earwig's sinful crime in the park. From his name and from 'the bynames was put under him' we may indeed gauge that 'our old offender was humile, commune and ensectuous' (29.30).

NOTES

1 See Adaline Glasheen, *A Second Census of Finnegans Wake* (Evanston, 1963), p. 193
2 See *A Wake Newslitter*, No. 3, June 1962, p. 2
3 Sigmund Freud, *The Interpretation of Dreams*, trans. A. A. Brill (New York, 1950), p. 245

Robert F Gleckner

BYRON IN FINNEGANS WAKE

By now it has been demonstrated amply and clearly that a number of the major figures of English literature had an enduring influence upon James Joyce and his writings–culminating in his enthronement of them, their works, characters, and lives as major elements in *Finnegans Wake*. Swift, Sterne, Shakespeare, Milton, Blake, Wilde, and Shaw are perhaps the most prominent. I should like here to add another to the list, although his pervasiveness in the *Wake* is not so easily seen because of his confusion with several other figures and because he is more often represented by his characters and poems than by his name. I speak of Lord Byron, for whom Adaline Glasheen, for example, even in her revised and enlarged *A Second Census of 'Finnegans Wake'* (Evanston, 1963) lists only a few references, including those to Childe Harold and Don Juan. J. S. Atherton in *The Books at the Wake* (New York, 1960), however, has provided additional evidence of Joyce's use of Byron and Byronic material by listing some twenty references–to Byron by name and to *Childe Harold's Pilgrimage*, *The Corsair*, *The Giaour*, 'Maid of Athens', and *Don Juan*. But since it is not to his purpose, Mr Atherton makes no suggestion as to the pattern of these references, nor of course has he pursued the Byron-Joyce relationship particularly. In this essay I propose to do both of these things.

On the surface of it *any* relationship between Joyce and Byron seems fairly unlikely (there is not a single reference to Byron in Mason and Ellmann's edition of *The Critical Writings of James Joyce*, for example)–until one becomes aware of the several clues and hints in Joyce's earlier work and in his life. Stanislaus Joyce, for example, remarks, almost by the way, about Joyce's 'boyish hero-worship of Byron'[1] and then testifies that Stephen Dedalus' quarrel with three of his school friends in *A Portrait of the Artist as a Young Man* was a faithful rendering of an incident during Joyce's own schooldays.[2]

This section of *A Portrait* begins with a discussion by Heron, Boland, Nash, and Stephen about their reading and their fathers' libraries. Nash, 'the idler of the class', declares Captain Marryat the greatest writer; Stephen, with Heron half-mockingly prodding him, names Cardinal Newman as the greatest prosewriter. Heron then advances Tennyson as the best poet and Nash agrees. 'Tennyson a poet!' Stephen cries. 'Why, he's only a rhymester!' The greatest poet is 'Byron, of course', and to Heron's accusation that 'Byron was a heretic and immoral too', Stephen retorts hotly: 'I don't care what he was'. With this his three adversaries attack him, trying to force him to admit 'that Byron was no good', and when Stephen stubbornly refuses they leave him 'half blinded with tears, clenching his fists madly and sobbing'.[3]

The incident is significant in several ways, for in addition to the establishment of Byron's preeminence in the mind of the young Stephen-Joyce,[4] the command of Stephen's tormentors for him to 'admit' that Byron was no good is associated quickly in Stephen's mind with Heron's earlier command (punctuated by blows from his cane) to admit they had 'found him out' in his attraction to Eileen,[5] and with the implication of his admission of heresy in his class essay.[6] Further, not long before this collocation of events Stephen attempts his first love poem, writing on a piece of paper which he heads, automatically, with the Jesuit motto (A.M.D.G.) before jotting down his title: 'To E—— C——.' 'He knew it was right to begin so for he had seen similar titles in the collected poems of Lord Byron.'[7] The connection is clear between Byron's supposed heresy and immorality and the accusations, implicit and explicit, of Stephen's, and this is accentuated by Joyce by having Stephen think of love, a woman, a poem, Byron, and the Jesuits all mixed together. We should not be surprised, then, at Stephen's romantic-erotic Byronesque, Childe-Haroldesque, farewell to Ireland at the end of the novel: 'The spell of arms and voices: the white arms of roads, their promise of close embraces and the black arms of tall ships that stand against the moon. . . . They are held out to say: We are alone. Come. . . . And the air is thick with their company as they call to me, their kinsman, making ready to go, shaking the wings of their exultant and terrible youth.'[8]

This youthful identification with Byron, while never lost, I think, does mellow at the same time into Joyce's more mature appreciation of Byron's power as an artist. As late as 1930 we find Joyce writing a series of letters to George Antheil, the composer, discussing the possibility of making an opera of Byron's *Cain*, which Joyce thought 'could be the basis of a fine libretto'.[9] With John Sullivan, the great tenor, particularly in mind, Joyce begins to cut and rework *Cain* into the libretto, suggests to Antheil the voices needed.[10] About two months later, he reports that he has completed his adaptation of Act I, is ready to start on Act III, and is more than ever convinced that Act II must be done choreographically. Obviously enthusiastic about the possibilities, he writes that *Cain* is 'A magnificent subject never treated before in opera, the work and name of a great poet and the most remarkable operatic voice in the world of our time.'[11] And in the same letter, from Paris: 'People here think that the combination Cain-Byron-Antheil-Sullivan with myself thrown in as scissors-man would be the greatest event in the artistic future.'[12] In January of 1931, however, Antheil has cooled considerably on the subject and Joyce allows him to withdraw gracefully, if he will 'allow [Joyce] to offer poor Byron and poorer Sullivan elsewhere'.[13]

Contrary to Stephen-Joyce's implication in the *Portrait* that Byron the man (heretical and immoral) and Byron the poet should be kept distinct, in *Finnegans Wake* Joyce, in general, goes the way of almost all Byron critics and confuses Byron with his characters, most particularly Childe Harold and the Corsair-Giaour figure. But while it must be admitted that there is some literary criticism (or at least implicit judgment) of sorts in the *Wake*, Joyce's main purpose involves not literary criticism but patterned allusiveness, analogy, parallelism, as well as, of course, contrasts and antinomies. And it is in these terms that most of the Byronic material in the *Wake* can best be studied.

Andrew Cass, in his generally unsympathetic article, 'Childe Horrid's Pilgrimace' (*Envoy*, V, 1951, pp. 19-30), is certainly correct in pointing out that the general confusion between Joyce and his main characters is analogous to the confusion of Byron and his characters. Joyce's 'flight' to Europe, Cass suggests, is parallel to Byron's self-exile from England in 1816; and Joyce's indictment of the Irish as 'the most belated race in Europe' and of Ireland as an 'inhospitable bog' has obvious parallels in Byron's denunciation of England and the English. Cass concludes, somewhat acidly: 'Byron is also Joyce's exemplar in having borne through Europe the pageant of his bleeding heart while the impressed continentals counted every drop, but here again he is outdone by Joyce in bitter antagonism to the people whom he blamed for his exile.' But Cass's essay is severely limited and not a little colored by his antipathy to Joyce (as well as to Byron) and especially to *Finnegans Wake*—and he goes no further with his most suggestive analogies.

Mrs Glasheen describes Humphrey Chimpden Earwicker as follows: 'Adam ybounden, one-eyed, grousing, stammering, defending—a hump of guilt, like Christian's, on his back. Then suddenly he is up and abroad, disguised as this man, that man, everyone, nobody.'[14] One of these disguises, I submit, is Byron and somewhat oddly, Childe Harold. The simplest evidence of this relationship is Joyce's habitual association of Byron with drinking, just as HCE is a tavern owner, and Finnegan the hod-carrier falls, drunk, from the ladder only to awaken at his own wake when he is accidentally splashed with whiskey. Also HCE is deformed, just as Byron was deformed, the humpback of the former and the twisted foot of the latter both being visible signs of their 'guilt'; both HCE and Byron are involved in a sexual scandal, the ingredients of which range from indecent exposure and peeping-Tomism to homosexuality and incest; and finally, and perhaps most important, the transformations of HCE, as well as those of the other main characters of *Finnegans Wake*, are analogous in Joyce's mind to Byron's transformation of himself into his main characters.

Although Byron was not a great drinker, Joyce seems constantly to think of him as such in *Finnegans Wake*, perhaps partly for the purpose of associating him with Brian Boru, the Irish hero-king who fought off the Danes in 1014 in freedom's cause much as Byron fought for Greek freedom from the Turks, and whose name is easily punned upon (Boru–brew). Joyce's clearest use of this connection is 563.12, 'lordbeeron brow' (with German *brau* as well as a hint of Joyce's relating of Byron and Cain, about which I shall have more to say below). Other examples occur in a passage describing Finn MacCool, HCE's epic alterego: 'boor browbenders' (130.2)[15] and 'bier through the burre in' (130.12); in the tavern scene, expectedly: 'Brewinbaroon' (316.9); in Jaun's section: 'And the Beer and Belly and the Boot and Ball? Not forgetting the oils of greas under that turkey in julep' (464.28–9, the last phrases a reference to Byron's 'Isles of Greece' in *Don Juan* and thus to Byron's aid in the Greek cause against Turkey).

More important than the drinking theme is Joyce's identification of HCE with Childe Harold. Although it is difficult, perhaps finally impossible, to dissociate Byron's character from Harald I and Harald II of Norway, Harald Harefoot of the Saxons, and Harold II of England,[16] there is strong evidence for seeing Childe Harold in all the Harold references in the *Wake*. The key identification is on p. 41, following references to such other literary figures as Shelley ('epipsychidically'), Swinburne ('swimborne'), Shaw ('shaw'), Yeats ('yoats'), Wilde ('wilde'), to Byron's poem 'Maid of Athens' ('meed of anthems here we pant'), to Byron by name (though Henry James Byron, author of the play *Our Boys*, is also intended), and to drinking ('the hogshome they lovenaned The Barrel'). The identification is in the phrase 'Ebblinn's chilled hamlet'–HCE's initials in reverse, with reference to Krafft-Ebbing's works on sexual perversion and hence to the sin in Phoenix Park (in that chilly hamlet of Dublin), to Byron's perversion and guilt, to Hamlet's guilt and melancholy, and to Childe Harold's dissolute past, guilt, and melancholy. This initial identification of HCE and Childe Harold is corroborated later by 'Hunkalus Childared Easterheld' (480.20), and perhaps by Byron himself in his Preface to Cantos I and II of *Childe Harold's Pilgrimage*: 'It is almost superfluous to mention that the appellation "Childe", as "Childe Waters", "Childe Childers", &c., is used as more consonant with the old structure of versification which I have adopted . . .' (cf. Joyce's 'Haveth Childers Everywhere'–535.34–5). In Shaun's dialogue with the people, Childe Harold remains as HCE and Byron, his creator, is properly seen as Shem-Joyce, the writer of the letter, of *Finnegans Wake*, of 'his pillgrimace of Childe Horrid', in which, as Andrew Cass suggests, the pageant of the bleeding heart is displayed–or, as Shaun puts it in the *Wake*: 'him, the cribibber like an ambitrickster' (423.5–6) writes the document.[17]

Although there are no other instances in the book where HCE and Childe Harold are as neatly combined, there are a number of supporting references to Harold-Humphrey, to pilgrimages, and most especially to the farewells indulged in prior to the pilgrimages. For the first we have, for example, 'Harold' twice on p. 30, both times with Humphrey (lines 2, 21), 'Haromphreyld' (31.8–9), 'Haromphrey' (32.14), 'Haraldsby, grocer' (i.e. Harold the Great–139.34), 'Then old Hunphydunphyville'll be blasted to bumboards by the youthful herald' (375.5–6), 'They were harrowd, those finweeds' (527.3–4),[18] 'herald' (597.34–though I think this means simply a herald), and 'horild haraflare' (610.3). This last, though probably a reference to Harald the Fairhair, must also be Childe Harold since it echoes the earlier phrase, 'pillgrimace of Childe Horrid'.

The references to pilgrimages are somewhat complicated by the fact that Joyce makes frequent use of most of the suras of the Koran, one of which is entitled 'Haji', meaning pilgrimage.[19] While this allusion is certainly possible in the word 'pilgrimage', it is difficult not to see Childe Harold present as well, especially in 51.29 where 'pilgrimage' is preceded by 'bryns', in 'making pilscrummage to whaboggeryin' (305.33),[20] in 'That's our crass, hairy [cf. pili-, the combining form meaning 'hairy'] and evergrim life' (455.13–14),[21] and in 'your photophoric pilgrimage to your antipodes in the past' (472.17–18).

The farewells are even more interesting, and more Byronic, for most of them are based upon Byron's 'Fare Thee Well' to his wife, the first two lines of which are:

Fare thee well! and if for ever,
Still for ever, fare thee well.

They are automatically associated, then, with Byron's farewell to England, Childe Harold's 'last Good Night' as he leaves England, Don Juan's farewell to Spain, Joyce's farewell to Ireland – and hence also with the theme of exile. Thus when Shem first 'testifies' about his father's history-making episode in the park, as Pegger Festy he 'declared in a loudburst of poesy, through his Brythonic [which includes Britannic and Byronic] interpreter on his oath . . . why he left Dublin' (91.3–4, 21–2). More pertinent is Jaun's parting from his sister Issy after delivering himself of his Poloniesque 'sermon': 'So for e'er fare thee welt!' (454.1–2), 'Fare thee well, fairy well!' (454.27–8), 'With the Byrns which is far better and eve for ever your idle be' (455.2–3), 'to aye forever' (455.22). Yawn later picks up the same theme: 'Hunkalus Childared Easterheld. It's his lost chance, Emania. Ware him well' (480.20–1); and at the inquest we find: 'Tell Queen's road I am seilling. Farewell, but whenever! Buy!' (521.35–6).[22]

It is into this context of farewells that Joyce's several references to Byron's 'Maid of Athens' fit – for that poem too is of parting:

Maid of Athens, ere we part
Give, oh give me back my heart.

Further, I think it clear from the second reference in the *Wake* to the poem[23] that Joyce intended to identify the maid of Athens with Anna Livia Plurabelle, thus further consolidating the HCE-Harold-Byron relationship. This reference occurs as one of the washerwomen by the river Liffey, gossiping and washing the dirty linen of people's lives, refers to ALP in these terms: 'Then a toss nare scared that lass, so aimai moe, that's agapo!' (202.6–7), echoing Byron's Greek refrain in 'Maid of Athens', 'Zoe mou, sas agapo'. Finally, in Jaun's sermon to the little girls of St Bride's Academy, which in its emphasis on chastity and infertility stands in direct contrast to ALP (and hence to the maid of Athens), he advises, in a parody of the halting, hobby-horsical rhythms of Byron's prudish satire, *The Waltz*:

Mades of ashens when you flirt
spoil the lad but spare his shirt!
Lay your lilylike long his shoulder
but buck back if he buts bolder
and just hep your homely hop and heed no horning
but if you've got some brainy notion
to raise cancan and rouse commotion
I'll be apt to flail that tail for you till it's borning. (436.32 ff.)

I have arranged the lines as doggerel verse to show more clearly that the parody is extraordinary, combining as it does not only Byron's bad verse in *The Waltz* (including the flat conjunctions and the limp opening words in the line) but that peculiar blend of prudery and sexual abandon one finds in Byron's make-up, and the 'homespun' advice to the girls to dance their own wholesome steps rather than the lewd jostling of the waltz. That Joyce knew Byron's poem well is shown by his reference in the above passage to 'horning' (Byron's nom de plume in *The Waltz* is Horace Hornem) and by the clear reference later which incorporates the same paradoxical attitude toward sex: 'And the volses of lewd Buylan, for innocence!' (435.10).[24]

Three additional elements in this leit-motif or pattern deserve comment. After Jaun concludes his sermon, Pandarus-like he urges his sister Issy into the arms of her brother Shem, 'like boyrun to sibster' (465.17), that is, like Byron's incestuous relationship with his half-sister Augusta Leigh, which led to the marriage scandal and to

Byron's farewell to England. The second reference is more complex
– and more problematical: 'Lood Erynnana, ware thee wail!' (469.
21). Capitalizing on the contrast between Jaun's sermon and the
character of ALP, Joyce combines here (among other things I'm
sure) Jaun's farewell to the girls and his sister Issy, the 'lewd' Lord
Byron already established (435.10), the 'lewd' Anna Livia (in Jaun's
terms, of course), the farewell to lewd Ireland by Joyce, the farewell to England by Byron and Childe Harold, the farewell to ALP
and hence to the maid of Athens, and Byron's 'Fare Thee Well' to
his wife, as well as to Augusta. Though the song, 'Sweet Innis-
fallen, fare thee well', may be present here,[25] the Childe Harold context is strengthened by the misquotation two lines earlier from
Childe Harold's 'Good Night': Byron's 'Farewell a while to him and
thee' becomes Joyce's more appropriate 'Farewell awhile to her and
thee!' The third additional farewell reference is tied to these via the
Byron-drinking theme as well as the rhythmic 'Fare thee well! and
if for ever', and relates Byron, properly, to his friend Thomas
Moore: 'Gulp a bulper at parting and the moore the melodest!
Farewell but whenever . . .' (468.27–8). The particular reference, I
think, is to Byron's famous farewell *To Thomas Moore*, which
begins:

My boat is on the shore
And my bark is on the sea;
But before I go, Tom Moore,
Here's a double health to thee!

And ends:

With that water, as this wine,
The libation I would pour
Should be – peace with thine and mine
And a health to thee, Tom Moore.[26]

There remains one other pattern of reference to Byronic material
in *Finnegans Wake*, and this is the Corsair-Giaour theme. This
theme is clearly a reflection of Joyce's sense of his own outlawed
condition – not only from Ireland but from society, the world – and
his developing in *Finnegans Wake* what Harry Levin calls 'The
Language of the Outlaw'.[27] This sense of isolation, of aloneness, of
being a kind of Ibsenian 'Enemy of the People', permeates Joyce's

work as it does Byron's; and both men had an extraordinary sense of their own power, uniqueness, mind, far above that of the ordinary man. But while Joyce tends to associate this kind of man, as Shelley does in *A Defense of Poetry*, with the poet-bard-artist, Byron sees him as a man of action, fighting the world or fighting against the forces of oppression everywhere. Joyce clearly recognized this kinship, but he also recognized Byron's difference from him—and it is this double recognition which gives rise to the outlaw theme in the *Wake*.

The references are not difficult to find: though a few are questionable, most of them occur in a context bolstered by allusions to other outlaws or pirates—or to Turks, Mussulmans, Armenians, Albanians, and the like. Byron's Giaour is mentioned a number of times, and I shall here merely add four to those cited by Atherton:[28] 108.17 ('giardarner'), 228.33 ('gheol ghiornal, foull subustioned mullmud'). This is a most interesting reference since it combines the outlaw-pirate theme with the sexual-guilt[29] and Childe-Harold-pilgrimage themes. The opening phrase recalls John Mitchell's *Jail Journal* and Oscar Wilde's *Ballad of Reading Gaol*, and the last phrase refers to Wilde himself via the name he adopted after his trial, Sebastian Melmoth, and therefore to *Melmoth the Wanderer* by C. R. Maturin, which deals with a man who sells his soul to the devil and wanders in misery and melancholy over the face of Europe. Also 312.32 ('jewr of a chrestend'), 329.31 ('All Sorts' Jour').

Equally interesting are the references to corsairs, which also bring together not only the outlaw theme in general but also the theme of guilt (being cursed)—and hence the Cain-Abel theme—and the Childe Harold theme. Atherton lists five references to corsairs[30] but since he does not comment upon them, I shall do so when it is pertinent (the only references I can add to his are 89.11–'It was corso in cursu on coarser again' and 626.28–'Corsergoth').[31] The first important appearance of the corsair is, significantly, as part of Joyce's initial characterization of Shem: 'he was an outlex between the lines of Ragonar Blaubarb and Horrild Hairwire' (169.3–4). Ragnar Lodbrok was a Viking chief; Blaubarb, while obviously but curiously Bluebeard, must also refer to Blackbeard the pirate as well as, perhaps, to Barbarossa whose name means 'red beard'. This last is the more likely since Joyce, with the resurrection theme of *Finnegans Wake* in mind, surely knew of the legends which had it that Barbarossa would not lie quiet in his grave and had to be buried several times. 'Horrild Hairwire' is Childe Harold as 'the wandering outlaw of his own dark mind' and by virtue of the pun Harold Coarsehair (corsair).[32] The pun is corroborated by 'coarsehair highsaydighsayman' (323.3) and by 'if I find corsehairs on your river-frock and the squirmside of your burberry lupitally . . .' (444.27–8), which combines corsairs with the Barbary Coast pirates, the fierce Berbers, and predatory wolves. In one of Taff's descriptions of Butt-Shem, Joyce also associates his corsair with '*Draco*' (343.2), the Athenian law-giver whose very laws the corsair breaks; with Sir Francis Drake whose early career was little short of piracy; and also, perhaps, with Byron's Conrad (anagram of '*Draco on*' – 343.2) in *The Corsair* and with his Lara ('*Lour*' – 343.2).[33] Finally, the guilt-curse-exile theme is reflected in 'the kongdomain of the Alieni, an accorsaired race, infester of Libnud [i.e. Dublin] Ocean' (600. 10–11).

We have, with this, come full circle, for with the hint of Cain, accursed, brow-branded, and outlawed, we must also recall 'lordbeeron brow' and Byron's mark on the forehead, as bright as Shem's, Joyce's, and all other defiers of God and law. As Ellmann says, in *Cain* 'Byron anticipated Joyce's interpretation of Cain and Abel as light-bringing Shem and conforming Shaun.'[34]

Finally, as a kind of postscript, I might add that, especially since Shem is Byron the poet as well as being the Childe Harold aspect of Byron the man, Shaun seems to me properly the Don Juan side of Byron, associated by Joyce with lewdness, sexual conquests, as well as with a certain peculiar, but strong, sense of prudery. One is tempted to see Jaun immediately as Juan, though the evidence seems to point rather to the legendary Spanish Don Juan or to Don Giovanni. Still Joyce's habit is to combine rather than to separate, and Byron as Don Juan and hence as Shaun-Jaun seems to me as likely a pair as HCE-Childe Harold. My only 'proof', however, and it is hardly conclusive, is the one time Joyce spells Jaun's name 'Juhn', calling him 'that dandyforth'[35] and alluding, perhaps, to Byron's peculiar Anglicized pronunciation, Jew-an. With or without *Don Juan*, however, I think it clear that Byron and his works play a much greater role in *Finnegans Wake* than we have heretofore seen, and that he should be allowed to take his place beside those other great English writers who have contributed, unwittingly, to a modern masterpiece.

NOTES

1 Stanislaus Joyce, *My Brother's Keeper* (New York, 1958), p. 99 [112]
2 See also Richard Ellmann, *James Joyce* (New York, 1959), p. 40
3 *A Portrait of the Artist as a Young Man*, pp. 80–2 [82–4]
4 Ellmann asserts that this was not merely a youthful judgment: 'Joyce held to these opinions of Newman and Byron in later life' (*James Joyce*, p. 40n)
5 *A Portrait*, pp. 76–8 [78–80]
6 *Ibid*, p. 79 [81]
7 *Ibid*, p. 70 [72]
8 *Ibid*, p. 252 [257]. Ellmann corroborates this much of the connection between Byron and Joyce as follows: 'His own conflict with the Church, his plunge into callow sexuality, his proud recalcitrance in the name of individuality and then of art, his admiration for Parnell, for Byron, for Ibsen and Flaubert, his Parisian exile, all began to merge as parts of this central conception in which the young man gives up everything for art' (*James Joyce*, p. 153)
9 Letter to George Antheil, 7 September 1930, in *The Letters of James Joyce*, ed. Stuart Gilbert (New York, 1957), p. 292
10 Letter to Antheil, 23 September 1930, in *Letters*, p. 293
11 Letter to Antheil, 7 December 1930, in *Letters*, p. 296
12 *Ibid*
13 Letter to Antheil, 3 January 1931, in *Letters*, p. 297. In 1934 Joyce tried once more, this time to get Othmar Schoeck to write the opera based on *Cain* – in vain (Ellmann, *James Joyce*, p. 681)
14 *A Second Census of 'Finnegans Wake'*, p. 111
15 M. J. C. Hodgart and Mabel P. Worthington note that a nursery rhyme, 'Brow Bender', is also being alluded to here (*Song in the Works of James Joyce* [New York, 1959], p. 102)
16 Mrs Glasheen, for example, writes: 'I think that all Harolds and Haralds... are identified with [Harold II], but I do not exactly understand his significance to Joyce' (*A Second Census*, p. 109)
17 With this reference to the weeping melancholy Byron-Childe Harold, compare the following passage, in which Joyce pokes fun at the pose by seeing it as popular (yet at the same time tragic) comedy: 'at the movies swallowing sobs and blowing bixed mixcuits over "childe" chaplain's "latest" ' (166.13–14)
18 This remark is made *re* HCE's sin in the park. It may also be noted that Byron was a Harrow man
19 Atherton, in *Books at the Wake*, charts occurrences of 'haji' on pp. 347, 533, 571, and of 'pilgrimage' on pp. 51, 62, 312, 472, 483
20 Cf. Joyce's description of Ireland as an 'inhospitable bog', as England was to Harold and Byron
21 This last, of course, makes use of HCE's initials as well
22 Hodgart and Worthington see the following songs in these last three passages: 'Good-bye, Summer', 'It's Your Last Voyage, Titanic, Fare You Well', and 'Farewell, but whenever You Welcome the Hour' (*Song*, pp. 151, 155, 160)
23 The first is 41.10 in a context with Byron, HCE, and Childe Harold

24 That Joyce is alluding to *The Waltz* here is corroborated by the reference five lines later to *The Blue Danube* (435.15–'Blue Danuboyes')
25 Hodgart and Worthington, p. 153
26 Hodgart and Worthington index the song reference here as 'A Bumper at Parting' (p. 153). We should perhaps relate Byron's 'bark . . . on the sea' to HCE's dream-voyage, in which there is a clear reference to the famous ocean passage in *Childe Harold*: 'Rolando's deepen darblun Ossian roll' (385.35–6). The other reference to this same passage of *Childe Harold* associates HCE's awakening or resurrection, the song 'Roll, Jordan, Roll', and hence Anna Livia in her ocean disguise: 'his mighty horn skall roll, orland, roll' (74.4–5)
27 *James Joyce: A Critical Introduction* (Norfolk, Conn., 1941). Cf. Joseph Campbell and Henry M. Robinson, *A Skeleton Key to 'Finnegans Wake'* (New York, 1944), p. 12: 'Shem is typically in retreat from society, he is the scorned and disinherited one, the Bohemian, or criminal outcast, rejected by Philistine prosperity.' As many students of Joyce, I am particularly indebted throughout this essay to this book
28 Atherton's references are 68.18, 107.22, 305.3, 355.22
29 See also the following passage for another example of this connection: 'beauw or the bummell, the bugganeering wanderducken' (322.36–323.1)
30 323.2, 343.3, 444.27, 577.10, 600.11
31 Hodgart and Worthington index this as part of the song, 'Father O'Flynn' (p. 96)
32 Hodgart and Worthington index this as the song, 'There's Hair like Wire Coming out of the Empire' (p. 106)
33 Lara may also be present elsewhere in the *Wake*: 'laracor' (228.21), 'Kaledvalch' (Kaled was Lara's lover disguised as his page–241.12), and 'Laraseny' (618.31), here a police sergeant upholding the very laws Lara breaks
34 *James Joyce*, p. 640
35 473.10. Joyce no doubt knew of Byron's association with several of the prominent dandies of his time

James S Atherton

SPORT AND GAMES IN FINNEGANS WAKE

'Sport's a common thing' (51.21).
It has frequently been remarked that the local allusions form one of the major obstacles to the understanding of *Finnegans Wake*. Joyce seems to have expected his readers to be aware of every detail of his own personal experience. One element of this experience which is least likely to be understood by the usual reader of the *Wake* derives from the interest in sport shown by most of Joyce's fellow-citizens of 'the most phillohippuc . . . paùpulation in the world' (140.12). Most readers can translate this as remarking that the poor citizens of Dublin are horse-loving drunkards—assuming that 'hippuc' conflates hiccup and hippo. The difficulty arises when Joyce uses words or phrases of which the meaning can only be seen by those with some knowledge of horse-racing in the British Isles in the 1920s or of English cricket in the 1890s. An example of the sort of thing that can happen is 'didando a tishy' (232.31). The reader is expected to know that Tishy was an English race-horse which lost so often that a newspaper cartoonist, Tom Webster, began to use it as a comic character in his daily cartoon; it was usually shown with its front legs in a knot and its front hoofs wide apart. 'To do a tishy' was a catch-phrase used for a few months in 1922 meaning to fall with your legs in a tangle. One wonders why Joyce used such ephemeral material in such large quantities that his work is bound to become more difficult to interpret as time goes on.

Joyce's advice to 'Wipe your glosses with what you know' (304. F3) may be relevant here; he aimed at putting something for everyone into *Finnegans Wake* and it may be that the racing terms, and so on, are intended to give clues to the labyrinth to those who lack the knowledge to follow his literary and historic clues. The mind boggles at the prospect of *Finnegans Wake* being read by bookies, but I consulted a local bookie about some of the expressions that concerned racing. The first was 'from flagfall to antepost' (90.6). 'That's an Irish way of putting it,' he said. 'Antepost is before the flag has gone down. This fellow's working backwards.' And in fact Joyce meant to convey that the events described at this point 'during the effrays round fatherthyme's beckside' (90.7) are going backwards in time. A later variant of the phrase, 'From the fall of the fig to doom's last post' (583.22), is probably meant to include this reversal of time as one element in its complexity.[1]

Overt references to horse-racing begin with 'a priestly flutter for safe and sane bets at the hippic runfields of breezy Baldoyle' (39.1). Baldoyle is a race-course near Dublin. When 'W. W. goes through the card' (39.2), W. W. is presumably a jockey, for 'goes through the card' is still the normal racing term for winning every race on the program. 'Winny Widger . . . in his neverrip mud and purpular cap' (39.11) must be the same person. The 'purpular cap', presumably popular and purple and mud coloured, suggests a satirical intention which is supported by the phrase 'easily capable of rememberance by all pickersup of events national and Dublin details' (39.3). 'Dublin details' is quoting a newspaper headline for a column about Dublin race-horses; the Grand National is a very famous steeplechase but surely Joyce is mocking his horse-loving countrymen here and when he writes of 'events grand and national' (13.31). There can be no doubt about Joyce's intention at a later point when he writes of the 'trulley natural anthem: *Horsibus, keep your tailyup*' (498.6)–what it says is that the Irish national anthem should be 'Horsey, keep your tail up' not 'Soldiers are we'. Joyce's Shaun tells the girls to 'fight shy of mugpunters' (439.33). Mugpunters is the bookies' word for the ordinary uninformed backer of horses. As a slang phrase it dates back to the 1920s.

Usually horse-racing is referred to in the *Wake* as a generally known activity, an inescapable but somewhat unimportant background feature whose popularity is somewhat absurd. Joyce himself occasionally visited the races with his friends when he was in Ireland. Afterwards he often listened to the radio programs from Athlone, including those sponsored by the Irish Hospitals Sweepstake, which included traditional Irish songs and racing information. Horses, such as '*Boozer's Gloom*' (342.5) which ran frequently in the 1930s, were also mentioned on the B.B.C.'s London Regional programme which is named in the *Wake* as '*Loundin Reginald*' (342.33). But most of the references are to the Irish programs and 'our incomeshare lotetree' (191.18), or 'grandnational goldcapped dupsydurby houspill' (448.14). Both of these refer to the Irish Sweep and the second example seems to be objecting to the topsy-turvy sense of values that can find no way of dealing with social evils that does not involve a sport which is itself a source of social evils. It is punning on the names of three horse-races: the Grand National, the Ascot Gold Cup and the Derby. The Gold Cup is, of course, the race which Throwaway won on 'Bloomsday', and here shares the word which names it with a gold-coloured jockey's cap. Another phrase, 'the sport of oak' (448.24), comes from Oxford where 'to sport your oak' means to close your front door as a sign that visitors are not wanted because you are working. In the context, with a racing theme involved, it also refers to the Oaks, the most important of English races for fillies, but the passage is full of phallic symbols such as 'knobs of hardshape' (448.23), suggesting that the fillies are not there for the purpose of racing.

According to Freud, sport and games, like art and literature, are ways of sublimating sex. Joyce uses this theory with enthusiasm in the *Wake*, although it is applied less extensively to horse-racing than to any other form of sport. However, in 'The field is down, the race is their own' (583.7), there is an obvious analogy drawn between horse-racing and copulation. The passage 'this classic Noctuber night', with 'a racerider in his truetoflesh colours, either handicapped on her flat . . .' (481.28) makes the same analogy but perhaps needs the explanation that 'flat' races, which take place in the summer, include all the 'classics'. Joyce seems to be ridiculing the fact that for millions of people 'who speak the tongue that Shakespeare spake' the word 'classic' denotes the five chief English horse-races. The only other time that Joyce uses the word, according to Clive Hart's *Concordance*, is in the phrase 'the classic Encourage Hackney Plate' (39.5) which refers in even more obviously mocking terms to this usage and to the disproportionate attention paid to racing. In the *Wake* the theme recurs constantly interwoven with other themes. 'Peredos Last in the Grand Natural' (610.34), for example, combines a racehorse named Peredos with a pun on *Paradise Lost*, and *per* and the Greek *edos*, the seat of the gods, while 'Juva' who has money on a 'Tempt to wom Outsider' (*ten to one* and *tempt to womb*) watches the 'supremest' drink 'Wartar wartar' (610.20) that recalls Frank Power who had nothing to do with racing. Racing is, in fact, an inescapable part of the Irish background, and comes in *Finnegans Wake* for that reason.

Cricket is not a popular game in Ireland; the average Irishman's attitude is that shown in Shaw's *John Bull's Other Island*: 'Cricket! Is it bat and ball you mean?' Joyce played the game at Clongowes and, although he left that school when he was nine, his affection for the game is apparent in the brilliant evocation of the sounds of cricket practice on a summer evening which ends the first section of *A Portrait*: 'In the soft grey silence he could hear the bump of the balls: and from here and from there through the quiet air the sound of the cricket bats: pick, pack, pock, puck: like drops of water in a fountain falling softly in the brimming bowl.' And forming, one may add, an image of completion and content at the quiet evening close of a full and happy summer day. There was no cricket played at Belvedere, but James forced his brother Stanislaus to help him practice. Stanislaus wrote: 'He still took an interest in the game when he was at Belvedere, and eagerly studied the feats of Ranji and Fry, Trumper and Spofforth. I remember having to bowl for him for perhaps an hour at a time in our back garden in Richmond Street. I did so out of pure goodness of heart since, for my part, I loathed the silly, tedious, inconclusive game'.[2] Stanislaus goes on to note that James Joyce 'detested rugby, boxing and wrestling' and used an account of a boxing match in the Cyclops episode of *Ulysses* 'to associate violence and brutality with patriotism'.

Although cricket was Joyce's favourite game as a boy, his attitude seems to have altered as he grew older and it is used in *Finnegans Wake* in a satirical way. Joyce seems to have resented the almost religious respect which many English people have for the game and associated this aspect of it with those platitudes about 'keeping a straight bat' and 'playing the game' which are sometimes regarded as the most unpleasantly hypocritical parts of the English character. Incidentally, the Western Brothers, an English music-hall pair who mocked this attitude in a song which they frequently broadcast in the thirties, 'Play the game, you cads!', are mentioned in the *Wake*. Or, to be accurate, Kenneth, the elder brother, gives his name as a substitute for Western in 'Normand, Desmond, Osmund and Kenneth' (514.2). In a correspondence in the *Times Literary Supplement* on 'Joyce and Cricket'[3] it was disclosed that Joyce took no interest in the cricket at Dublin University, but that his father was very interested in it and often talked about it. On the other hand it is well known that Joyce told Frank Budgen that he accepted him as an honest man because he looked like a former cricketer, Arthur

Shrewsbury. I have wondered whether this was, perhaps, a further test of Budgen's bona fides, for anyone who had been brought up in an English public school—as a foreign-office agent might be expected to have been—would have known that Arthur Shrewsbury shot himself on 19 May 1903, and might not have been reassured by the resemblance. However, a study of many photographs of Arthur Shrewsbury has finally convinced me that he did, in build at least, resemble Frank Budgen.

There is undoubtedly a considerable amount of satire on the English public-school system in the *Wake*. One of the most noticeable aspects of that system is its reliance on compulsory games—partly with the idea of distracting the boys' attention from sex. Stanislaus remarks, 'The occupation of boys, according to Meredith, is to be outdoor sports, for it is one of the principles of moral hygienics that these expel suprapatellar curiosities.'[4] Joyce would know both his brother's and Meredith's comments and had experienced the principle in operation. Cold baths are another aspect of this asexual regime. Joyce has fun about this when he describes the twelve-mile-long school of herring, 'all of a libidous pickpuckparty' (524.35) in 'cold water', the use of which 'may be warmly recommended for the sugjugation of cungunitals loosed. Tolloll, schools!' (525.4). 'Tolloll' combines 'Good-bye' (cf. 65.17) and 'Tell all schools', where the schools are the breeding herring and all educational establishments. The latter are to be told that their prophylaxis for sex provides vast scope for sexual activities.

Cricket is made by Joyce to provide a similar scope. The joke is, of course, that the popular English conception of a cricketer is that of a clean-living upright gentleman. Joyce chose cricket as the game to which, according to the Freudian theory, the principal act of copulation in the *Wake* was to be sublimated. The passage beginning 'Kickakick' (583.26) is crammed full of cricketers' names. The list begins with 'robberer. Cain-' (583.28) which combines two people. The first is Robert Abel, mentioned later in the paragraph as 'bobby abbels' (584.2), who in a Test Match in Australia in January 1893 opened the batting and 'carried his bat' through the innings to score 132 not out. This is being referred to again in 'he carries his bat!) nine hundred and dirty too not out' (584.23). 'Cain' is C. Stewart Cain who was the editor of Wisden's *Cricketers' Almanack* from 1926–33. Joyce probably took all the information he uses in this paragraph from these editions of Wisden, and Cain must be 'wisden's bosse' (584.16) who is acknowledged again at the end of the paragraph. One meaning of 'robberer. Cain-' is probably 'robber of Cain'–a joking acknowledgement of Joyce's borrowings. The next three well-known cricketers are Tarrant, Brand and Askew, 'trumbly' is H. Trumble, and 'ringeysingey' is K. S. Ranjitsinhji (also named in 'ranjymad' (10.9)). Spofforth, Duff, Tyldesley, Tunnicliffe are all cricketers named in the lists of 'Births and Deaths of Cricketers' in Wisden: so are Studd and Stoddart, Trott, Trumper, Lord Harris, Blackham, Iremonger, Daer, Buller, Parr, W. G. Grace, Pooley, Merriman, Lillywhite and Hobbs. They are named in this paragraph in the order I have given them and are nearly all of the period 1880 to 1903. The phrase 'norsery pinafore' combines the names of two players: Nosworthy and Pinney, with 'the nursery', which is the name given to one end of the famous London cricket ground, Lord's. This ground is being mockingly referred to earlier in the phrase '*Cumberer of Lord's Holy Ground*' (71.34). As the headquarters of the M.C.C.–the Marylebone Cricket Club, which is the ruling body over English cricket–Lord's is the headquarters of English cricket. The other London ground, the Oval, is brought into this passage in 'ovalled' (584.19); Hambledon, where cricket is said to have started, is named in 'hambledown' (584.18). Many cricket terms are used. 'King Willow' (583.28) is a name for cricket; 'elbiduubled', in the previous line, is L.B.W.'d–that is, put out 'Leg before wicket'. The phrase is used again in 'Leg-before-Wicked' (434.10). The 'duuble' is a verbal play with the sound of the name of the letter W. 'We're parring' (584.8) includes a reference to George Parr the first English cricket captain, another 'Old Parr'; 'empsyseas' says M.C.C.'s.

There is, of course, always another, and usually bawdy, meaning to be found for each of the terms from cricket. Often these, like the allusions to Lord's, form part of a complicated series or pattern of jokes spreading over the entire book. The word 'block' has several meanings. According to Partridge's *Dictionary of Slang and Unconventional English*, 'block', as a verb, means to have intercourse with a woman. The 'block' or 'block-hole' in cricket is the hollow made at the crease, or line behind which the batsman stands, to mark the place where the bat will be rested. One notices 'that battery block' (25.17) and 'enjoyed by many so meny on block at Boyrut season' (229.34), in both of which the cricket is almost submerged. Another example, 'hand of the christian ... has a block at Morgen's and a hatache all the afternunch; plays gehamerat when he's ernst . . .' (127.29), apart from the triple pun (a hatter's block is being used), is interesting as concealing the name of Christian Morgenstern: Christian . . . Morgen . . . ernst. The last syllable is obeying the command 'turn' which can be heard in the original syllable 'tern'. Again Joyce is playing the game of doing what the letters tell him—just as in L.B.W. mentioned earlier. But the total meaning of the phrase 'her old stick-in-the-block' (583.26) should now be clear. A yorker, as in 'after the rising bounder's yorkers' (583.36), is a fast ball aimed straight at the block-hole, and intended to bounce on the block-hole.

Another theory about games which would have appealed to Joyce is the anthropological one which maintains that children in play re-enact the history of their race. Joyce must have read the article on 'Children's Games' in the *Encyclopaedia Britannica*, probably the eleventh edition, from which he took so much other information on all kinds of subjects. This article would direct him to Alice B. Gomme's *Children's Singing Games*, and her *The Traditional Games of the British Isles* where this theory is put forward and the words and music are given of many of the games which are used or alluded to in the *Wake*. The theory is intertwined with the various versions which Joyce makes of a sentence by Quinet in which he turns the wild flowers which Quinet says have survived the rises and falls of Empires into 'the lilts of children'.[5] As early as the first version of this sentence the children are playing at making love and war and death and resurrection with laughter and tears. Yet, much as this idea must have suited Joyce's ideas about the cyclic nature of history, it is never allowed full play, for on every occasion when it is used it is combined with the Freudian theory of games as sublimations of sex. Even when 'Darkies . . . play non-excretory, anti-sexuous, misoxenetic, gaasy pure, flesh and blood games' (175.30), the meaning on the surface is contradicted by the interwoven allusions. 'Gaasy pure' refers to 'Gassy' Power's Dinka boy, whom he bought naked to release from slavery, and dressed in a long robe in an attempt to make him look decorous which was foiled by the urchin's trick of standing on his head every ten minutes to uncover his nakedness.[6] The rest of the passage is largely based on Norman Douglas's *London Street Games*, for which Joyce seems to have used the second edition, published in 1931. 'Misoxenetic' presumably means stranger-hating and says, if obscurely, what it means, but the other adjectives are used ironically for many of Douglas's games are really ways in which some London children used to abuse and mistreat strange children they had caught on their territory. '*Prisson your Pritchards and Play Withers Team*' (176.2) is Joyce's rendering of 'Piss in your britches and play with the steam', a 'game' in which, according to Douglas's young informant, a strange boy would be blindfolded and told to await a surprise. The surprise, which gave its name to the game, was not 'non-excretory'.

One of the games described in *Children's Singing Games* (Vol. I, pp. 22–7) is 'Jenny Jones'. This is a variant of the 'Angels' or 'Colours' game which Joyce uses (see *Letters*, p. 295). The last verse ends:

Poor Jenny is dead, dead, dead,
Poor Jenny is dead, you can't see her now.

There's red for the soldiers and blue for the sailors,
And black for the mourners of poor Jenny Jones.

The rhythm is reproduced, as Hodgart and Worthington point out,[7] in the passage beginning 'Poor Isa sits a glooming' (226.4). The notes by Alice Gomme say that 'In some versions, too, an important incident, that of "ghost", or spirit of the dead occurs. The dead Jenny, after the burial is accomplished, springs up and pursues the mourners, who scatter in all directions.' This death and resurrection is, of course, the central theme of *Finnegans Wake*, so we see that the games of the children are again imitating the activities of past generations. Another game drawn from Gomme, 'Old Roger is dead and gone to his grave', which becomes 'poor Glugger was dazed and late in his crave' (240.3), has the same theme, for Old Roger gets up and attacks his mourners. The name Jenny which appears frequently in the *Wake* probably includes Jenny Jones each time it is used. Glugger ties up with Uggugg from Carroll's *Sylvie and Bruno*, and the entire series of games with the Lewis Carroll theme. Alice Gomme's name is probably given in a paragraph about 'old Dadgerson' in the words 'invented gommas' (374.10) and also in 'the game for a Gomez' (545.31).

When 'The youngly delightsome frilles-in-pleyurs are ... drawens up consociately at the hinder sight of their commoner guardian' (224.22), Joyce is describing how, as A. B. Gomme says, the girls huddle together behind the girl who is playing the part of 'mother' so that the child whose turn it is to guess cannot see them. When Glugg, who is Shem, starts to play it is insinuated that he should 'make peace in his preaches and play with esteem' (225.6). In other words he is the unwanted stranger and the children wish to play unpleasant tricks on him, and there are other, darker implications. Another game from Gomme, 'Looby Loo', has become well known in the last few years; it is played (226.26-9) in the same passage. There are many other children's games mentioned but I must pass on to other aspects of the theme.

It is to be expected that when Joyce decided to introduce games he would introduce all the games he could find. Sometimes so many things are inserted into the *Wake* that the original matter is almost concealed. An examination of the Mss. of early versions shows that details about horse-racing which look as if they are the chief connotations in some passages are, in fact, late decorative additions. When Joyce first used the word 'Cesarevitch' (498.2), for example, it was as a part of a farcical list of important visitors and meant the eldest son of the Czar.[8] But the word reminded him of the race, run at Newmarket in October, which is named after the Cesarevitch Alexander III who was in England when the race was instituted, so Joyce brings in a number of other horsey details. The St Leger, another important autumn race—this time named after an Irishman—and often linked with the Cesarevitch in 'the autumn double', the rhetorical term *hysteron proteron*, putting the cart before the horse, 'Isteroprotos' (498.4), and the '*Horsibus, keep your tailyup*' are all later additions to an aspect of a word which that word was not intended to convey in the first draft. Sometimes the games are part of the original draft and hidden by later accretions. One such underlies 'the hero, of Gaelic champion . . . with his sinister dexterity, light and rufthandling, vicemversem her ragbags et assaucyetiams, fore and aft, on and offsides, the brueburnt sexfutter . . .' (384.23). At one stage this read: 'The handsome sixfootwo rugger and soccer champion . . . with sinister dexterity he alternately rightandlefthandled fore and aft the palpable rugby and association bulbs.'[9] Here the Freudian theory of games is in control of Joyce's metaphors as the Association footballs, which are spherical, sublimate for Iseult's breasts, while the Rugby footballs, which are oval, do the same for her buttocks. But although I remembered reading this passage when I was studying the manuscripts I had some difficulty in finding it when I began looking in *Finnegans Wake* for games for this essay, and I do not see how anyone could pick up the allusions from the final version. Perhaps I should point out here that the ball used in English Rugby football is, though larger, of a much more gently rounded oval shape than that used in American football. Joyce refers to a Rugby football elsewhere when 'the rugaby moon' is among 'the cloudscrums' (449.34). The word 'rugaby' conflates rugby and rock-a-by, from the lullaby, and means gibbous. To return to the previous passage, 'the hero, of Gaelic champion' shows that Tristram has become a player of yet another kind of football: Gaelic football. Indeed Joyce seems at times to aim at presenting a confused blend of games.

The mixing of the games is sometimes funny, sometimes puzzling. Issy is confused at one point as to whether her young men play football or hurling. Hurling is a very ancient Irish game which, although its enthusiasts hotly deny it, strongly resembles hockey; but there are fifteen players a side as in English Rugby Union. Issy complains about 'that espos of a Clancarbry, the foodbrawler, of the sociationist party . . . and all his fourteen other fullback maulers or hurling stars or whatever the dagos they are. . . . He is seeking an opening. . . . Andoo musnoo play zeloso!' (144.5). 'He is seeking an opening' is often used by radio football-commentators to say that a player is trying to find a way to score; Issy, who seems to have a different end in view, has no doubt as to the nature of the opening sought. 'Zeloso' is Spanish for zealous; it also means 'hot' in the sense in which animals are said to be 'on heat'.[10] Here it probably includes pelota, a Basque game which is probably as ancient as hurling. But what the game is does not seem to matter much as what they are really doing is making love. Pelota is combined with chess at one point, although the two games could hardly be more unlike for pelota is probably the fastest ball-game in the world: 'pawns, prelates and pookas pelotting in her piecebag' (102.15). Here the other intruder's 'pookas' combine the Gaelic for a goblin or 'puck' with, from the context, the 'puck' with which ice-hockey, a game even faster than pelota, is played. In a later passage pelota is mixed with golf—and civil war between Guelfs and Ghibellines— and polo as 'Polo . . . and Plein Pelouta . . . ghimbelling on guelf-links' (567.35). Polo and playing pelota and gambling or gambolling on golf-links is one of the threads. The phrases I omitted include 'behowl ne yerking at lawncastrum' which words conceal bowl and yorking, from cricket, and a probable allusion to tennis in 'lawncastrum'. Joyce's childhood games at Clongowes, where teams had the names of York and Lancaster, come in by association with the other games and become mimic civil wars. In this way the two principal theories about games are constantly interwoven into all the references to games, and these seem to be mixed up with another theme: that the *Wake* itself is a game and includes all other games right down to such occupations as 'puny farting little solitires' (567.34), in the sentence before the one just quoted, which includes solid-tyred penny-farthing bicycles with the humble game of solitaire. Three sports, squash, tennis, and boating, are named together in 'our love tennis squats regatts, suckpump, when on with the balls did disserve the fain' (366.10), but perhaps it is in hunting that the quarry becomes most elusive. In a passage running for half a page from 'Gundogs of all breeds were beagling' (96.36) the beast pursued becomes a hare, an otter (from 'holt'), a rat, a badger, a bear, a hare again, then turns into a fox and is lost. The card players give little indication of the game they are playing but it seems to be solo whist. Joyce seems to be quoting phrases he has overheard from card players, for example, 'loyal six I lead, out wi'yer heart's bluid' (122.14)–where the 'heart's blood' would be the opponent's last trump card–and playing games with the words himself. Another example is 'ace of arts, deuce of damimonds, trouble of clubs, fear of spates' (134.7) in which his hero is the ace of hearts, the deuce–or the devil–of the demi-mondaines, or the two of diamonds, the three of clubs (from *treble*) and the person who causes trouble in clubs, and the four of spades or the fear of death to his enemies. Joyce himself is playing with the names of the cards. What the characters are often doing is playing at being shadows. 'The ombre players' (24.36) could be three men playing the eighteenth-century card game but they are attendants at a wake. Only three can play ombre; presumably the fourth old man is too remote from the rest to join in. But he is there at the football game when the score is 'Four ghools to nail!' (377.34) which combines four goals to nil with four ghouls to nail down. Some British football teams are named in the same passage. 'Partick Thistle agen S. Megan's versus Brystal Palace agus the Walsall!' (378.18) is what we are told the match is. But Partick Thistle is a Scottish football team from Glasgow; there is a team called St Mirren from Paisley in Scotland. Megan was a Welsh saint who has no football connection. Crystal Palace and Walsall are English football teams, apparently they are playing as a combined side for *agus* is Gaelic for 'and'. What is happening is that the Earwicker we are all dreaming about has reached one of his many ends; in a moment he will have eluded us, as the quarry in *Finnegans Wake* always eludes the hunters, by turning into somebody else. We will be dreaming of the arch-king Roderick O'Connor, but he will still be the same man in reality and we will be the same people with all our miscellaneous collection of information and our foolish obsession with sport and games. It is thus that the pursuing of any one thread in the *Wake* leads to the centre of the labyrinth.

I have said that all games are named, at least, in the book. There is not space to prove this, and little purpose would be served by giving an unreadable list of the names included. There is, however, one game which I have barely mentioned which seems to be treated in a somewhat different way from the others. This is lawn tennis. It may well be that Joyce was influenced solely by the fact that the word 'love' is used for zero when scoring at this game. Love, which according to Bloom is 'the opposite of hatred', is a key word in Joyce's vocabulary and he may be protesting at the tennis players' abuse of it. 'Love all. Naytellmeknot tennis!' (361.9) seems to support this interpretation. Perhaps it is as revenge for this that Joyce pokes fun at tennis. 'Tennis Flonnels Mac Courther' (452.9), which conceals the name Tennyson and sounds rather like Denis Florence MacCarthy, may be ridiculing tennis as well as its other contents; while 'A perspirer (over sixty) who was keeping up his tennises panted . . .' (59.33) also contains the suggestion that the game is rather ridiculous. So does 'soaking and bleaching . . . to deck my tennis champion son, the laundryman with the lavandier flannels' (214.25). On the other hand we are back to the usual Freudian interpretation with the final invocation of the maidens to Shaun: 'playtennis!' (470.20); for, after all, tennis is the game at which one starts, as Joyce himself has told us, at 'Love all'.

NOTES

1 'The fall of the fig' refers both to the fall in Genesis and the end of the world as described in Revelation, 6.13: 'The stars of heaven fell unto the earth even as a fig tree casteth her untimely fruits.' Another link between the two passages is that the stars are falling, 'skiddystars', in the 'flagfall' sentence
2 *My Brother's Keeper* (London, 1958), p. 61 [41]

3 Letters by the present writer and Gerald Brodribb, W. P. Hone and Eoin O'Mahony, *T.L.S.*, 9, 16, 30 May and 20 June 1952

4 *The Dublin Diary*, p. 91

5 *Letters*, p. 295. For the versions of the Quinet sentence see Clive Hart, *Structure and Motif in Finnegans Wake*, p. 238

6 See Frank le Poer Power, *Letters from Khartoum* (London, 1886), and my 'Frank le Poer Power in Finnegans Wake', *Notes and Queries*, September 1953, pp. 399–400

7 *Song in the Works of James Joyce*, p. 113

8 B.M. Add. Ms. 47482b, 83

9 Add. Ms. 47481, 94. An alteration, 'her palpable' for 'the palpable', was probably made when this version was written

10 Joyce's Spanish, like many of the languages he used in the *Wake*, is based on nineteenth-century dictionaries. For *zeloso* see, for example, *A Dictionary of the Spanish and English Languages*, M. Velasquez de la Cadena (New York, D. Appleton and Co.), 1854

J Mitchell Morse

ON TEACHING FINNEGANS WAKE

We must become as little children, for they have no difficulty with *Finnegans Wake*. They have no taste: they can enjoy good writing as well as bad. Only with time and teaching do they learn to prefer the bad. Our first job as college teachers is to unteach them: to restore their innocence: and for this purpose *Finnegans Wake* is uniquely effective.

The discovery that it is not altogether inaccessible comes as a surprise even to graduate students who have read Joyce's other works; to freshmen who have not heard of Joyce it comes as the sudden recovery of a paralyzed sense, for it gives them for the first time since their pre-literate childhood the experience of a purely literary pleasure. Before a child learns to read, he can enjoy good language if he has a chance to hear it: 'One misty moisty morning', 'Cross patch, draw the latch', 'Mistress Mary, quite contrary', and 'Rig-a-jig-jig and away we go'; but in the first grade he learns with Dick and Jane and their dog Spot that language can be a joyless thing; and twelve years later, having had his taste developed by Lanier, Longfellow, Whittier, Freneau, John Masefield, Alfred Noyes, Rudyard Kipling, James Fenimore Cooper, Walter Scott, Conan Doyle, Booth Tarkington, Anthony Hope and Rafael Sabatini, together with bleached and degerminated versions of Dickens and Hardy by the likes of the authors of *Dick and Jane*, he goes to college and asks his English teacher, 'Is Ayn Rand considered a good writer?'

There is no point in arguing with a person so horribly diseased. The only thing to do is to start curing him right away by exposing him to good language. Allopathy, I say. There are of course plenty of suitable specimens in contemporary literature – I may mention the description of Watt's clothes in Beckett's *Watt* (pp. 217–19), the account of the moon's passage in *Molloy* (pp. 51–2), some of Nabokov's stories, some of Nicolò Tucci's, some of Katherine Anne

Porter's—butI have found that the Prankquean episode of *Finnegans Wake* (21.5-23.15) works best of all.

It works so well because it presents an obvious challenge. One reading aloud suffices to show that it is not chaotic but has some kind of three-part pattern; after a second reading many students can see that the pattern is that of a fairy tale, and that in addition to the three main parts it has a coda, though they don't use that word; most of them begin to suspect that it has some meaning, if they could only somehow figure it out, and now and then one sees that the meaning inheres largely in the form, that to a large extent the form *is* the meaning. One said to me, 'This is like a musical score: the conductor has to know where the theme is and who has it and what he must do with it.' When a student reaches that point he is practically cured; for when he begins to think of what he reads in terms of form, he begins to have a sound base for literary judgment. I think, incidentally, that at least in the classroom we should avoid the word 'taste', a metaphor of unaccountable subjectivity that makes literary judgment analogous to a preference for one kind of ice cream rather than another and misleads us into believing that there is really no way to tell good writing from bad. If I believed that—if I believed that my pleasure in Joyce was not demonstrably more valid than a freshman's pleasure in Ayn Rand—I would not presume to teach the art of reading or the art of writing. To be concerned with form is to be concerned with something demonstrable: a purely literary quality in terms of which one piece of writing is better than another. Concern with form is the beginning of judgment; and for making even the most naïve students aware that there is such a thing, I have found the Prankquean episode uniquely valuable.

But *Finnegans Wake* as a whole is of course not for freshmen. It is for graduate students; and with them our purpose is not primarily to develop a consciousness of literary values but to gain some insight into the work at hand. *Finnegans Wake* immediately presents them with a stimulating paradox: for they discover that it is not by any means virgin territory, that it was not virgin territory even when Harry Levin and Edmund Wilson first explored it, that in fact (Joyce's weapons being exile, cunning and publicity) it was never quite virgin territory, that nevertheless it remains largely unknown, and that—like nature itself—it will always by nature remain largely unknown.

For it is not fixed. It does not stand still for our inspection. Like every living book, it is fluid and endlessly evolving. Socrates' argument in *Phaedrus* that what is written down is fixed, dead and defenseless—an argument that the very setting of the dialogue mocks with its altar to Boreas, its reminders of Achelous, and its flowing Ilissus—all symbols of the Athenian loquacity and of Plato's own art, a flashing, shimmering iridescence that cannot with any fidelity be represented by a black-and-white diagram—

Where was I? Ah. Socrates' argument against writing down our living thoughts, an argument all around which *Phaedrus* flows, a living refutation, is refuted by every living book, and most especially by *Finnegans Wake*, which every generation must begin anew and every reader must approach anew each time he opens it.

Naturally we don't undertake to read the whole book in a school term. At the first meeting I lecture, by way of introducing the subject; at the second we read rapidly and superficially a number of passages in different styles, to get an idea of the book's stylistic variety, to see how themes are modulated to different purposes, and to glimpse the order in their gay profusion; then we settle down to Book I, Chapter i, start reading it in as much detail as possible, and try to finish it by the end of the term. Sometimes we do finish it, sometimes we don't; in either case, we learn how to go about reading *Finnegans Wake*.

Between sessions we make use of all the guides and keys, all the lists of names, songs, words, books, themes and motifs, the *Newslitter*, *The Analyst*,[1] the *OED*, Skeat's etymological dictionary, Grove's musical dictionary, and all the lexicons we are equipped to use; but when we bring our findings together we find that the act produces a qualitative innovation as radical as the occurrence of life in a carbon compound. For reading *Finnegans Wake* is a collective enterprise of no ordinary kind: what takes place is no mere quantitative gathering and mechanical assembling of parts into larger units, but a blending of objective and subjective elements—a kind of communion—in which one person's information calls up from another's subconscious an inference that validates the conjecture of a third. Joyce has revived the magical function of the old bards and shamans, in what by convention we consider a most unlikely place, the seminar room. If it should suddenly begin to rain in the room, I suppose we would all be surprised; still, it just might. Certainly we generate something in the nature of a ritual atmosphere. It is not surprising that Joyceans drink Guinness and John Jameson, go on pilgrimages, and publish memorial volumes; the impetus to such pieties comes from the sacred texts themselves.

The pedagogical problem is to stay within the limits of the demonstrable, beyond which lies if not madness at least silliness, without discouraging those happy intuitive leaps that in the best scholarship sometimes precede demonstration.

Finnegans Wake lends itself most happily; for its art is only an elaboration of principles that began to appear very early in Joyce's work. As William York Tindall has pointed out, the word 'innumerous' in the last line of the poem 'From dewy dreams, my soul, arise', means both 'innumerable' and 'not numerous'; but it also suggests the Latin *innumerosus*, unmelodious, inharmonious; Joyce uses the word 'numerose' to describe Shaun's voice (*FW*, 407.17); and Tindall's observations on the disharmony of the last two lines of the poem support and are supported by my reading of the word.[2] In 'The Sisters', the handkerchief with which the paralyzed priest tries to wipe away the stains of spilled snuff is 'quite inefficacious'. The word 'ineffective' would have suggested the priest's physical debility just as clearly, but the theological word 'inefficacious' suggests spiritual debility as well, and also indicates the turn the narrator's mind has been given by the priest's instruction. Stephen Dedalus in the *Portrait* thinks of his raging sexual desire as 'the luxury that was wasting him'. 'Luxury' here is an anglicization of *luxuria*, the official name of the deadly sin of lechery; by using this obsolete meaning of a modern English word, Joyce makes more poignant Stephen's conviction of sin and also indicates very early the pedantic tendency of the boy's mind: there is a hint of self-mockery even here. These examples suggest that the early works are 'difficult' in essentially the same way that *Finnegans Wake* is difficult. The difference is one of degree: in the earlier works the difficulty is not great once we see it, but it is unobtrusive and insidious, so that we may miss a point without suspecting that we have missed anything; in *Finnegans Wake* the difficulty is both more obvious and more difficult, being compounded through a multiplicity of languages and elaborated with boisterous virtuosity.

Paul Valéry's twentieth-century Faust describes its magical quality quite clearly: 'I want to produce a great work, a book. . . . It would be an intimate blending of my true and false memories, of my ideas, of my previsions, of hypotheses, of valid inferences, of visionary experiments: all my diverse voices! A reader could enter it at any point and leave it at any point. . . . Perhaps no one will read it, but anyone who does will never be able to read another book. . . . I want to write it in a style of my own invention, which will permit me to pass miraculously back and forth from the bizarre to the common, from absolute fantasy to extreme rigor, from prose to verse, from the flattest platitude to the most . . . the most fragile ideas. . . . A style, in short, that will unite all the modulations of the soul and all the leaps of the mind; and which, like the mind itself, will sometimes run back over what it is expressing in order to feel itself being expressed and recognize itself as the will to expression, the living body of that which speaks, the awakening of thought, which is suddenly astonished that it could ever have been confused about anything, though such confusion is precisely its essence and its role.'[3]

That is unmistakably the style of *Finnegans Wake*. Mephistopheles calls it 'Mephistophelean'. But it is not one style but many; for its nature, as defined by its purpose, is multiplicity itself. We should expect it to be less a style than a medley of styles, and in merely talented hands to be perhaps unavoidably cheap. The charge of acrobatic cheapness was in fact one of the commonplaces of commonplace criticism in the early years of *Ulysses*; even serious critics have said that *Ulysses* ran chiefly to parody and pastiche; conversely, it was for a long time assumed that *Finnegans Wake* was written in one style; and even now we hardly know what to make of its variety.

What I make of it provisionally is an interpretation so unorthodox that I present it to my students—and now to the readers of this volume—with some hesitancy. Harry Levin's insight that the publican HCE could not be the dreamer because he lacks the education to have such a dream[4] gives us our clue: the narrator is always somebody who could be the narrator of the particular passage in question. I believe that just as in *Ulysses* each character thinks, talks and is described in his own style, so in *Finnegans Wake* every change of style indicates that another person, awake or half-awake or asleep as they sit up with the body, is dreaming or being dreamed about. They are all HCE. However, since they dream about each other, it is often difficult to tell who is the current dreamer or narrator and who is a character in his dream or narration.

This is the way we provisionally interpret I, i at Penn State. It seems to explain some things that need explaining. In the first place, though the book begins and ends in the middle of a sentence, the second half of the sentence (3) has a style so different from that of the first half (628) that it seems not to be spoken by the same person. The first half brings an intensely lyrical passage to a climax with the iambic rhythm of copulation: 'A way a lone a last a loved a long the' – at this point the coition is interrupted – one of Joyce's obsessive jokes – and the second half of the sentence has the tone of a lecture: 'riverrun, past Eve and Adam's, from swerve of shore to bend of bay, brings us by a commodius vicus of recirculation back to Howth Castle and Environs.' Perhaps what we have here after all is not one sentence but fragments of two different sentences, so that *Finnegans Wake*, like the world, ends in the dark nothingness from which it emerged, and what we have is not a circle but a relatively small visible segment of a large invisible circle or ellipse or spiral or repetitive scrawl. This view enhances the grandeur of Joyce's conception. However that may be, the incomplete sentence with which the book ends is certainly spoken by Anna Livia, and the incomplete sentence with which it begins is certainly not. At the end Anna is losing her identity in that of her father-husband-sons, and the professorial tone of the opening fragment comes from him: not from the river but from the sea, not from our great sweet mother but from our great bitter father. 'Mearmerge two races [flows of water], swete and brack' (17.24). The all-inclusive sea, our comprehensive Old Father Ocean (627–8), speaks with the voice of Shaun or Shem or Anna or Isobel or the Four Masters or the Twelve Apostles or Adam or Eve or Jonathan Swift or Brillat-Savarin or the Duke of Wellington: like the Neo-Platonic God of Dionysius the Areopagite or Nicholas of Cusa, HCE is Everybody and Everything.[5]

The first narrator, who talks as if he stood with a lectern before him, a map behind him, and a pointer in his hand, is most probably Shaun; learning is not inconsistent with Shaun's character, and the vulgar tone of the whole lecture seems to be his. On p. 8 he breaks off the lecture and takes us to the museum, where the janitrix or genetrix, Kate the Slop, Goddess of Battles, shows us through. However, since after we leave the museum Shaun still has us in charge, it is likely that he continues to be the dreamer all through the museum passage (8.9–10.23), mocking Kate as his literary ancestor Buck Mulligan mocks Mother Grogan. Likewise in the Mutt and Jute episode (15.29–18.16), it is not the voices of Mutt and Jute that we hear but the voice of Professor Shaun, composing an imaginary interview (something professors have been known to do) and putting into his characters' supposedly primitive mouths allusions to the Stone Age, strong and weak verbs, Viconian cycles, a Wagnerian song, Tacitus' history and Wood's coinage scheme. After Mutt and Jute the lecture proper is resumed, and with the exception of a brief passage in which Shem speaks (19.31–20.18), is continued until Finnegan wakes (24.15). At this point it is suddenly broken off, the style changes abruptly, and what follows is not a lecture but a series of impromptu speeches by people at the wake, urging Finnegan to lie down and accept death, telling him that he would not care for the world as it is now, assuring him that procreation, building and destruction are being carried on as usual by his descendants, and comforting each other with the brave notion that not they but he 'will be ultimendly respunchable'–that he is Adam and God but they fortunately are not.

To determine who each of these deluded souls is would require a long, detailed stylistic analysis–which I for one, having other things to do, shall not undertake at any time that I can foresee. But I hope that others will agree and be moved to do it. Doubtless it would be a collective undertaking. In the reading of *Finnegans Wake*, everybody teaches everybody else.

NOTES

1 *A Wake Newslitter*, edited by Clive Hart and Fritz Senn, Department of English, Newcastle University College, Newcastle, New South Wales, Australia; *The Analyst*, Department of English, Northwestern University, Evanston, Illinois.–Ed.
2 *Chamber Music*, ed. William York Tindall (New York, 1954), pp. 199–200
3 Paul Valéry, *Mon Faust*, (Paris, 1946), pp. 48–50. My translation
4 Harry Levin, *James Joyce: A Critical Introduction*, (Norfolk, 1941 and 1960), p. 175. Clive Hart, in *Structure and Motif in Finnegans Wake*, pp. 78–82, discusses various conjectures as to the dreamer's identity. I see no necessary conflict between the single-dreamer and multiple-dreamer theories. The woman who invited Davin in for the night and the girl who tried to sell Stephen flowers were one and two and more than two
5 In his lecture on Shakespeare in *Ulysses*, Stephen Dedalus makes the same point: 'We walk through ourselves, meeting robbers, ghosts, giants, old men, young men, wives, widows, brothers-in-love. But always meeting ourselves' (213 [273])

Nathan Halper

THE DATE OF EARWICKER'S DREAM

(A) PRELIMINARY NOTES

1 Let us first confirm–there have been some doubts–that this is Earwicker's dream. A dream concerns its dreamer. The book deals with Earwicker's anxieties. If this book is a dream–the dream is Earwicker's.

2 The people in a dream are aspects of its dreamer. No matter who they are, he lurks behind each of them. In his dream, a dreamer is everyman.

Any man is everyman. Some, however, fill this role more efficiently than others. This applies to Earwicker. What he is, what he has, what he says or does, have been chosen by Joyce. Any detail of his life has been carefully machined so that it is like a gear, turning with minimum friction in a maximum of patterns.

3 We have a set of mirrors. Each of them reflects the others. Each is reflected. But, since they are all set at different angles, any one may show some aspect more clearly or completely than any of the others.

The day of the dream is one of the mirrors. It will help us to understand what there is to see in the others. But, conversely, we must look at others before we are able to determine this date.

4 Man is a *man*. Opposed to beast. He is a man. Not a woman or a boy. He is the man of the house. The husband: the father. The head of his family.

There are other meanings. Man–opposed to master. (There is such a servant in Earwicker's house.) Man–a nameless fellow: an impersonal pronoun. A counter in a game–one that someone else is playing.

The word acts as a control. It requires him to be *manly*. It also keeps him aware of its latent possibilities. It implies that he is aging–that his powers are declining.

5 As a dreamer, he's a father. The maker of his dream.

As a dreamer—he is tired. He has used the best part of his day. He fears he is losing his vigor, his authority.

6 The morning will refresh him. His son will renew him—But his hopes are only another face of his fear. The energy will not be his. The son is going to inherit *his* power, his vitality. His son will replace him, as he, the dreamer, replaced his own father.

7 In his dream, a dreamer seeks to release his tensions. Yet he cannot admit that the tensions exist.

Thus—he tries to speak. But he does not wish to hear. He carefully portrays his fear. But makes it unrecognizable.

In his dream, a young man asks Mr Earwicker the time. Another tries to make his way into the pub. The threat is always muted. Or happens to somebody else: in a different time and place. (During the Crimean War, a young Irishman, Buckley, shoots a Russian general.)

8 The younger man is not only Earwicker's son. He is Earwicker himself. He is pushing his own father. Equally, the older man is not only Earwicker. He is *his* father.

H. C. Earwicker is poised between the future and the past. He is his son; his father. The killer and the killed—sharing in the guilt of one, the fear of the other.

9 But the father is authority. Any time that it is breached, the son kills his father. This sin is a metaphor for every sin. This particular guilt a metaphor for every guilt.

The father is the *status quo*. Any time it is changed—the son kills the father. This act—this change—is a metaphor for every change. The particular fear a metaphor for every fear.

In that sense—every dreamer is a son: every dreamer is a father. A son feeling guilt. A father feeling fear. In that metaphorical sense, a dream, every dream, is basically about a son who kills his father. On a naturalistic level, the only one who can dream it—in all its implications—is a middle-aged man. A man like Earwicker who is afraid that he is aging.

10 It's every dream. He dreams it every night.

But, on this level—it is a particular night. Just as the dreamer is an ordinary man, this is an ordinary night. It is the end of an ordinary day. One that fades into the multitude of days.

74 THE DATE OF EARWICKER'S DREAM

But, like every day, it has its peculiarities.

It has its quiddities. For the purpose of this book, they are the optimum quiddities. They give this day a part, a role, in a maximum of patterns.

They make it the optimum day for Mr Earwicker's dream.

(B) THE DATE OF HIS DREAM

1 It is after World War I. The father-image, England, is about to lose his place to the United States. New England. Capitalism is being threatened by the Russian who, incidentally, has just murdered his own father.

2 Specifically, the year is 1922. In Dublin–scene of the *Wake*–English rule is giving way to a new Irish state.

H. C. Earwicker meets a Cad. When the Cad addresses him in Gaelic, Mr Earwicker is frightened. He fears that the young man is a gunman and is going to destroy him.

Here Earwicker is England. The Cad is Irish. He shows signs of being American and Russian. But–notably–he's Irish.

3 In the world of books, the year had a similar significance. In 1922, James Joyce published *Ulysses*. T. S. Eliot, *The Waste Land*. In this context, Earwicker is the generation of writers who already are recognized. The generation of Yeats. The Cad is Joyce. To a lesser degree, he is Eliot.

These two writers were literally called Bolsheviks–The Cad is a Russian. An American: an Irishman.

4 In 1922, Irish papers were full of gunmen. That year, in April, Mrs Joyce and the children paid a visit to Ireland. At one point, they were in a line of fire.

Joyce behaved like Earwicker. It was not merely that his family was threatened. He actually insisted that the bullets were meant for him.

In 1922, he began to work on his book.

5 In *Ulysses*, there is a meeting between father and son. Joyce is not only Dedalus. He is Bloom, the father, husband–the not-too-successful breadwinner that Dedalus is going to become.

Bloom is a younger version of Everyman. Unlike Earwicker, he is not yet afraid of the future. He is taken with Dedalus. The young man brings a new meaning to his life. He himself will be renewed.

Leopold Bloom is thirty-eight: an age Joyce reached while he was working on *Ulysses*. In his new book, everybody is older. The significant age is forty. On 129.32, Man is a cricketer whose stumps are pulled at eighty. The arc of his drive is forty. On 68.19, Earwicker is Arcoforty. Earlier, the Prankquean goes for a forty years' walk. This decisively changes the nature of Tristopher and Hilary.

In 1922, James Joyce was forty.

6 He is echoing Dante. In extending the life-span from seventy to eighty, he, too, is able to place his *Commedia* 'in the middle of this journey of our life'.

7 A Saturday night. The sun is about to rise. The week is about to end. Sunday is about to shine.

He is aware of sounds. They go into his dream. He is aware of his body: his wife's body beside him. They also get into his dream.

In the morning, he's aware of the changes in light. On p. 593 (the beginning of Book IV) the first words are, 'Sandhyas! Sandhyas! Sandhyas!' Or – *inter alia* – 'Sunday! Sunday! Sunday!'

8 Winter, too, is at an end – the sun is about to move into the equinoctial Ram. The day will be larger than the tired night. But, for the moment, there is a parity.

In Chapter Fifteen, the dreamer is asprawl on the Hill of Uisneach, the center of Ireland. In Time, as well as Space, he is at the hub. Poised between the Son and Father – yet partaking of each – he is the Spirit that mediates between them.

9 A night, any night, is the counterpart of its day. For this exemplary dream, it is fitting to have a time when they are literally equal.

This is a book of antinomies. Man-woman, Shaun-Shem, young-old, good-evil, right-left, space-time, law-liberty, have-have not, matter-will, justice-mercy, dove-raven, hill-river . . . day-night . . . It is full of counterparts that are opposite and equal.

On this list, day-night is the only pair we can numerically measure. It becomes a gauge by which to measure others. The time when they are equal is the time when Shaun and Shem, young-old, right-left – it is the schematic time when all opposites are equal.

10 In the first eight chapters, he tends to dream of things that happen in daylight. In the next eight, of things that happen at night. Near the end of Eight – the middle of these sixteen chapters – we have a sunset. The last word of this chapter is, 'Night!'

Such a structure is consistent with it being the equinox.

On p. 213-'the dusk is growing'. A few lines later, we have six o'clock bells.

This is also consistent.—But it is rather tricky.

11 On the day of equinox, the sun—ideally—should be setting at six. Ideally. At Greenwich. And if there were no atmospheric distortion. In Dublin, the sun sets around 6.30.

Joyce is always careful about such matters. It is the dreamer who is not so precise. He knows, in general, that it's time for the equinox. The sun should set about six. He goes by his impression. When he dreams of the sunset—he has it happen at six.

On the naturalistic level, the hour is wrong. But, on this level, it is what Earwicker would dream.

12 When he meets Earwicker, the young man is surprised to learn that it's earlier than he thinks. When another young man tries to get into the pub—it is later than he thinks.

Joyce uses Earwicker's mistake as a part of this motif. He also uses it to show that it is the schematic time, the symbolic time when all opposites are equal.

13 It is Lent.

If he wants to give advice to his teen-age daughter, it takes the form of a Lenten lecture. In his fear that he is losing his authority, he dreams that the sermon is given by his son.

He is conscious of this season as a preparation for Easter—That is an image of his fate. The Christ who will rise is his own son. The man of sorrow, the Christ who will be crucified, is Earwicker himself.

The drinking in his pub is a Last Supper. The customers are the Apostles. Four old loiterers are the Evangelists.

14 When he actually dreams of death, it applies to somebody else. On the manifest level, it is not he, it is the son who sets on a *via crucis*.

Even so—he does not evade his fear. The young Christ: Osiris: the young men in World War I—they are all of them dead. This becomes an image of his own sterility. The vitality is gone.

What is left are the four old men, the historians, analysts, the critics—*explicators*—who keep chivvying the corpse.

15 Christ died on a Friday. He rose on Sunday. On Holy Saturday, he went down into Hell.

Falling asleep is dying. Waking is a resurrection. The period between them is a Holy Saturday. A descent in the Underworld is a description of dreaming. In the dream of Dante, his descent into Hell also happened on Holy Saturday.

The phrase *felix culpa* keeps running through Earwicker's dream. This is from the hymn *Exultet*.

O felix culpa! O happy fault of Adam that enables God to manifest the glory of the Redemption. That allows him to show forth the modulations of his universe in all its infinite diversity.

By extension, it is the fault of every subsequent Adam. The sin, the guilt, of Joyce, of Earwicker. The cause, necessary cause, inescapable companion, of time, of change, discovery and creation. The happy fault that arms him, that gives him the fulness of his life, that allows him to work out the plenum of his dream, his art.

This hymn is chanted on Holy Saturday.

16 As we have seen, the dream is on a Saturday in Lent. This brings up a possibility that the actual day is Holy Saturday itself.

Easter may come on the 22nd of March. That puts Holy Saturday on the day of equinox. This would be welcome. But it happens rarely. The last occasion was in 1818–1913 is possible: they were one day apart. For our purpose, however, 1913 has no other allurements.

In 1922, Easter fell on the 16th of April. This puts the Saturday four weeks away from the equinox. If we are to choose between them, there are several reasons why we would pick the latter. In the middle of April, the sun, in Dublin, sets close to 7.30. Mr Earwicker has little reason to have it happen at six. ... At the equinox, he may think about Easter. On Holy Saturday, he is less likely to think of the equinox. (Especially, if it is four weeks in the past.)

Also, in the morning, he is conscious of Sunday. He is conscious of the sun. All through the dream, there is a prefiguring of Easter. But, in the morning–even when he hears the bells–there is no sense that it finally has come.

It is still in the future. Our day is the equinox.

17 We are not in the clear yet. In 1922, the equinox was not on Saturday. 21 March–the equinox–was on a Tuesday.

18 The equinox is the day the sun crosses the equator. The literal meaning of equinox is 'equal night'. It is commonly believed that, on this day, night and daytime are equal. (Even Webster's and the *OED* believe it.)

But this is not the case. That is–not precisely. It is true, on the equinox, the lengths of the night and daytime are close. They are very close. But there are days when they are even closer.

The 21st is the day the sun crosses the equator. The astronomical equinox. But Joyce is more concerned with the literal meaning. His interest is in a day when the opposites are equal. He is searching for an equal night: one that is twelve hours long.

In 1922, the interval between dusk on 18 March and sunrise, 19 March, is the night that comes nearest to his requirement. The 18th is a Saturday.

This is the time of Mr Earwicker's dream.

II

ADDITIONAL NOTES

1 Thom's *Dublin Directory* tells when the sun rises and sets each day. These charts take up 24 pages. They come early in the book. (In 1922 they began on p. 4.) Thus, they are something that one is likely to notice even if one only opens this book at random.

If he wanted such information, Joyce would have known it was there. If he was looking for anything else–it was easy to come across this. There is too much of a tendency to think he knew everything. But it required no highly specialized knowledge to know that, on the equinox, day and night are unequal.

The 1922 book explicitly makes this distinction. If he looked at the entries for September, Joyce would have seen that, on the 23rd, the caption says 'Autumn Equinox'. And, three days later, it says 'Equal Day and Night'.

2 There are a number of allusions to events that happened later in the year. This suggests that the date is early. If he knew about the burning of the Four Courts in June or the assassination of Michael Collins in August, that would seem to indicate that the dream came after these events.

There also are allusions to things that came even later. Yeats got the Nobel Prize in 1924. Is this the date of the dream? Shaw got it

THE DATE OF EARWICKER'S DREAM 79

in 1926. There is a mention of John Sullivan, the singer. Joyce did not meet him till November 1929. There is a reference to his eye-doctor, Vogt. He knew him in 1930.

Joyce began the actual writing in 1923. It may have taken a while to decide on the details. No name seems as immutable as Anna Livia Plurabelle. Yet, in the early drafts, he played with forms like Bessy Plurabelle Earwicker. However, we may assume that, by the time he began to publish extracts, 1924–5, he knew his cast of characters and was able to fix the place and the time. It is not easy to believe that, in the 1920s, he was working on a dream that was going to be dreamed in 1930. Nor is it likely that, once he settled on a day, he kept revising it, moving it into the future, altering it, year by year, every time he thought of a new allusion.

I am not saying that he had a good reason for putting Sullivan or Dr Vogt into his text. I am saying he did have a reason. Good or bad, the reason would apply to his mention of Collins or the fire in the Four Courts.

3 A dream is largely visual. Freud says it is like a rebus, a picture-puzzle. Each element of the picture represents some word or syllable. But, in *Finnegans Wake*, this process is reversed. The medium is words.

The words do more than serve their usual purpose. They not only describe the pictures. They reflect what the pictures are trying to express. The ambivalent feelings, the contradictory meanings. And, like a dream does, they show all of these at one time.

Then, having done it–they have to do it again. A dream repeats itself. It has few themes, but continues to worry them. It always says the same things, but finds an amazing variety of ways to say them– or rather, to conceal them. Joyce uses his words to show both of those worlds. A teeming world of concealments, and a teeming world that they are trying to conceal.

Joyce needs words which will allow him to do this. New, unusual words. And uncommon meanings, uncommon associations, for daily usual words.

His area of reference tends to become universal. This is what it should be. (His dream is every dream. The dreamer every man.) To make it more universal, he tries to fill in the gaps. He adds vocabularies, languages. He reaches new provinces. He gets new eruditions, new snippets of pedantry.

How does the dreamer know the things that Joyce does?
The question is natural. But it misses the point.
The dreamer does not dream these words. His medium is pictures. The words are those of Joyce. They are a way, an economical way, possibly the only way, of giving the sense–and senses–of the dream.

4 When he uses events that are later than Earwicker's dream–he does it for the same reasons. They help in its understanding. They make it more universal.

The universal, however, resides in the particular. The words have many meanings. But, at least one will always go back to Earwicker. There are many people. But, on one level, they are the members of his family. On another, they are facets, aspects, phases, of Earwicker himself. Their struggles are a mirror for the rivalries in his family. They are the struggles in himself.

They are the world around him. They watch him, praise and blame him. They belittle and exalt him. They threaten or reassure him. But, on another level, they are the doubts in Earwicker himself.

The allusions range through space. But there is one frame of reference in which they always relate to one particular place. A town, a house. Even a particular body, turning in a particular bed.

In a similar fashion–they make contact with eternity in a particular time.

5 March 1922. Troops begin to leave. The Royal Constabulary is starting to disband.

English rule is giving way to an Irish state. This is the interval: the period between them.

The Irish group is splitting. The sons were united. They were the Son in the war against the Father. They are going back to a separate identity. They are ready to resume the Battle of the Brothers.

This is also an interval: a period of transition. Their passion–for the moment–is in the General Elections.

6 Irish papers–and their readers–are taken up by two topics. One, the Elections. The other is the violence.

Hostility between the factions of De Valera and Collins has not yet gone into murder. But there are aggressions. A few times, open war has only just been averted. There is trouble in Ulster. Headlines tell of 'fiendish' acts against Catholics in Belfast.

Nearer home, the gunmen are killing soldiers or constables. All through March, the journals are reporting their shooting. In Dublin, in Tipperary, in Galway, Waterford, Cork. While evacuating the barracks. While in a hospital. While they are going to Mass.

7 They are Authority. The Earwicker. The father.
As *English* soldiers: *Royal* Irish Constables: they are doubly the father.
When he meets him, Earwicker thinks the Cad is a gunman. His own garments—kepi, belt, jackboots—are of a military nature.
He feels that he is like the constables and soldiers.

8 There are, also, allusions to voting.
In his review of the *Wake*, Edmund Wilson noticed their presence. But he took them to mean that the dreamer himself had once run for office. It is more likely that—like Joyce's father—he had worked in a campaign. But, even if some of the allusions are memories, they are dragged in from the past by what is happening at present.
On p. 111, the letter found in a dump—the archetypical Letter—says 'the hate turned the mild'.
The heat has turned the milk. The *hate* has turned the *mild*. The gentleness: pity—
The hate has turned the milk. The human kindness.
After this, it refers to the 'general's elections'.

9 When Joyce makes allusions to the situation in Ireland, he is using material that is already in the dream. Mr Earwicker knows what Joyce does. He has read the same items: he has heard the same rumors. He is equally agitated—and for similar reasons.
But, a few months later, the situation is different.
The Elections are held. The Courts are shelled—A burning of records—A sequence of reciprocal killings. The death of O'Connor—The ambush of Collins.
These are things the writer knows—but Earwicker doesn't. And yet, this is the sort of trouble he fears. He may not anticipate this gunning, that bombing. Yet they are a part of the danger he foresees.
They cannot get into the dream. However, Joyce may use them. They may get into the book. He describes Earwicker's fears in terms of things that happened and confirmed it. They give a weight to his anxiety. A grain: an edge. A rough, tangible edge.

10 When Michael Collins got killed, a scrawl appeared over Dublin. 'Move over, Mick! Make room for Dick!'

Variations of the phrase drift through *Finnegans Wake*. 'Move up, Mumpty! Mike room for Rumpty!' 'Stand up, mickos! Make strake for minnas!'

On a literal level, this is no reference to Collins. That came later than the dream. In order to make sense, it needs no reference to Collins. The dreamer thinks that he will be supplanted. 'Move up! Make room!' is a natural expression of his fear.

Yet there is a relationship. A reference to be exploited. By his play on the phrase, Joyce has the use of an overtone.

A body on a country-road . . .

We feel the taste of Earwicker's fear.

III

(A) AN ALTERNATIVE

1 The first actual writing Joyce did on *Finnegans Wake* was a draft of the passage now on pp. 380–2. After closing, an innkeeper drinks what his customers left in their glasses.

His name is not yet Earwicker, but he is recognizable. He is our protagonist. Like him – he is Joyce, soaking up the driblets of knowledge, the disparate leavings of tradition.

Like him, he is Ireland. (All his drinks are Irish.) There is also a sense of the befuddled innkeeper as the British Empire. Even in the early version, the odds and ends he has absorbed add up to a 'gill or naggin of imperial dry and liquid measure'.

This irrational activity is the end of his day. It is a prelude to his dream. Joyce, who is always alert to a ritualistic gesture, has begun with a passage that has a special importance.

There may also be a significance in the day he chose to do this.

2 He began on a Saturday. 10 March 1923.

It is possible, however, that he was not so much concerned with the day of the month as with its place in the movable pattern of Easter. 10 March preceded Laetare: the Fourth Sunday of Lent.

In 1922, this was equivalent to the 25th of March.

3 The 25th is Lady Day.

In the system of relationships Joyce uses in *Finnegans Wake*, night is to day as woman is to man. Night – and its dream – are the

womanish side of man. Lady Day is a day for Earwicker to dream.
It is the day of the Annunciation.

A tradition held it is the date of the Crucifixion. Another early tradition put the Resurrection on this day. There was also a belief that this was when the world itself was created.

In Rome, it was the equinox. It was, also, Hilaria: the resurrection of Attis.

4 In 1922, the next day was Laetare: the middle Sunday of Lent. It is a break in the severities. Restrained rejoicing is mingled with austerity.

Hilaria is less restrained. The celebration takes the form of a carnival. A release of restriction. Universal license prevails. As in a dream-people go in disguises.

A day for a 'funferall'!
In the context of Lent-so is Laetare.

5 Hilaria may be roughly translated as Joyce.
Laetare is rejoice.

6 It is hard to think he did not notice the conjunction. Or that, having seen it, Joyce was not tempted to give this week-end to the dream.

A year later, however, the union had separated into its component parts. If, having chosen this day, he now wanted to start on its anniversary, he had a choice between 25 March and the day preceding Laetare. In 1923-this day was the 10th.

7 The 10th is more of a concealment.

A dream lulls its dreamer. It is able to reveal because it manages to sound as if it's talking about something else. It hides the fact that something is revealed.

Joyce is doing what the dream does.

He began on the 10th because the time of his dream was 25 March -25-6-in 1922.

(B) OCULI SUNDAY

1 Not long after he made his gesture, Joyce changed his mind about the date. He kept the day of the week. The month: the year. But he set it earlier. He decided on 18 March-18-19-1922.

2 There is no great difference between these days. The arguments I have adduced in favor of one are, in the main, as valid when they

are applied to the other. He was thus able to move from the 25th to 18th with no major change in plan. But if this is so, it required no compelling reason. All he had to do is feel that, here or there, it meant a measure of improvement.

3 The sleeper fears the equinox. It is a divide: a hinge. Its turning is the time when his son is going to replace him. The 21st is the equinox. Joyce moved his date from a bit later to a few days earlier.

If other things are equal – the early date is better. It is when the fear is sharper.

The anticipation is worse than its realization.

4 The 21st is the equinox. The 18th, we have seen, is the time of actual parity.

The 25th has charms. But they are too straightforward. The 18th is better. It is the more devious. It does what the dream does.

It engages in misdirection.

5 The third Sunday in Lent is Oculi Sunday. It takes its name from the introit of the day. *Oculi mei* . . . my eyes. If Earwicker begins his dream on the 18th of March, it runs into this morning of Oculi.

In the opposite pairs that Joyce has in the *Wake*, Shaun is the Eye. His brother the Ear. A corollary to this is that Shaun is the good eye. Shem is the bad eye.

6 There are more allusions to eyes than have hitherto been noticed. Any such allusion usually implies a play on the homonym 'I'.

The I's repeat the pattern of his eyes. In any man or group – any Earwicker – Shaun is the I that this particular Earwicker likes to think of as his good I. He is the right I. Shem is the left I. The gauche. Sinister.

The story of Earwicker is the story of his I's. The struggle: the seesaw: the dialogue between them.

7 On one level, the book is about the writer himself. A bad eye: a weak eye. The adjectives describe not only his eyes. They give his picture of himself. They apply equally to Shem. A bad, weak I. Poor I. The troubled, the troubling, rejected, disaffected. The weary I.

The have-not I.

This is the side of Earwicker that makes his dream. The bad eye: dark eye – night-eye.

The inner I.

The first pages are an overture: a statement of the themes that will be developed in the book. They have no less than five allusions to eyes.

Joyce began these pages in the fall of 1926. The first draft had only one of the allusions. The second draft had two. By winter, there were four. This, however, does not mean that eyes grew important only as he worked on this passage. An overture must wait until the writer is definite about his themes. (He cannot weave the strands before he knows what they are.) He began the overture after more than three years of writing. It was a statement of the themes that, in that period, had formed themselves. If his first draft had a reference to eyes, any reference–even one of them–it means that they already were significant. When he kept adding such allusions, he was only giving the eyes an attention that was their due, an emphasis that was compatible with the importance that they had gained before this.

Once he began to deal with Earwicker's duality, the pun I-eye was sure to suggest itself. That his own were bad made this doubly certain. I would surmise that he saw this pun and knew early in the course of his labor the uses he could make of it.

8 In 1923, he began the actual writing. In July–four months later–he finally came to the subject of the equal, opposite brothers. This was the last of four isolated pieces. They were not fragments or tentative preliminary sketches. From the first, he had in mind their incorporation in the text. As he wrote to Harriet Weaver, they 'are . . . active elements and when they are more and a little older they will begin to fuse of themselves'. In a slightly expanded but not too different form, the episode is found on pp. 611–12.

It is near the end of the dream: the book. It is morning. Sunday. That is–it is Son–day. That the Son has risen reminds Earwicker of Easter. Notably, the Easter when, according to tradition, there was a debate between St Patrick and the druids.

When he reconstructs the episode, his sons get into the picture. Shaun takes the part of Patrick. Shem is the arch-druid. He is also Berkeley. (In his letter to Miss Weaver, he speaks of the two debaters as Patrick and Berkeley.)

The topic is significant. Berkeley wrote a treatise on vision. In this debate–the model of their debates–Shaun and Shem present two opposing theories of vision.

9 They both are bishops. Even if only by adoption, they are both Irish. They have birthdays in March. In 1922, these days were in the same week. (The week that ended on the 18th of March.)

If Patrick needed a counterpart, he was a plausible choice. This would lead Joyce to his treatise on vision. It is possible, too, that he thought of it earlier. It was the treatise on vision that took him to Berkeley. Either way—whichever came first—this would have led him to consider the possibilities of Oculi.

When, on 10 March, he began his actual writing, he was thinking of Laetare. But, by July, he shifted to Oculi. When—in the overture—he made his references to eyes, it was, *inter alia*, to establish the fact that the time of his dream was the week-end of Oculi.

10 I have been offering reasons why he may have made a change. Which is not to say that he actually made it. The proof, if any, should be in the text itself.

Let us do some research. *A Woman of No Importance* was in Dublin on the 20th. The work is mentioned on p. 158. Is this what we are asking for? A hint? A clue? If so—to what? The performance came between the two alternative days. Is he looking back? or forward?

It is also possible that this is mentioned only because it is by Wilde. (He is a type of Earwicker. Many of his works are mentioned.)

A play, *Peg of my Heart*, was at the Gaiety shortly after the 25th. Another, *The Scarlet Pimpernel*, was at the same theater a little before the 18th.

Which is the one that matters?

On p. 564—by the vice-regent's lodge, there is a Pimp-Parnell. On p. 143—the dreamer thinks of his daughter. She is a Peck-at-my-Heart. All through *Finnegans Wake*, Joyce keeps mentioning plays. He was always looking for allusions to Parnell: he was looking for analogues to Isobel. He may have thought of these plays and used them even if they were not current.

In sports, the evidence is similarly inconclusive. The Grand National Steeplechase was held in March. The papers were full of it. We may infer that the dreamer was aware of it.

One of the horses, Drifter, was owned by Mr Widger. On p. 39, when a steeplechase is described, the jockey is Widger.

This determines little. There are the same objections. It may well mean that the dreamer noticed the name. He put it into his dream. Yet, at most, his use points to the period in general. Not to a specific date.

Also – again – Joyce may have used it anyway. A widge is a horse. The rider and horse, the widger and the widge, are opposite and equal.

Neither should we draw conclusions from the emphasis on Patrick and the occasional allusions to St Patrick's Day. That this is on the 17th of March does not necessarily mean that the dream is on the 18th. No more does the emphasis on the Annunciation and Angelus mean that this day is the 25th of March.

Or the attention to Parnell that it is the 6th of October.

11 If, at some moment, Mr Earwicker is thinking of a particular day, this – by itself – does not make it the day on which he happens to be dreaming. The point may be precisely that it isn't.

Just as the writer managed to weave into his text the names of plays and players, battles, cities, rivers – he tries to get in allusions to a number of days.

We may go even further. He has worked in allusions to all books of the Bible, all plays by Shakespeare or *Irish Melodies* of Moore. It is conceivable that, in one way or another, he has managed to hint at every day of the year.

12 This is only partly for the purpose of misdirection.

He has a second reason. It is every dream and he's taking steps to show that it happens every night.

The universal, however, has its home in the particular.

It is a specific dream. He is taking pains to give it a specific night: a house in which its universality may most efficiently reside.

13 There is misdirection. Joyce not only uses the dream's own devices. He adds a few the dream has never thought of. Twenty-five years have passed since the *Wake* was published. (Over forty since a fragment was printed.) Scholars have given to the book their most ingenious devotion – Understanding still is not complete.

We move in a landscape of varying degrees of light and varying degrees of darkness. Unavoidably – we see things that are not there: do not see things that are. Some of the shadows lift. Yet things we thought were clear once again become uncertain.

This adjustment to experience, re-adjustment to experience, this continuous re-evaluation – this relationship between the book and reader is an essential part of this book.

Joyce, then, has to balance between concealing and revealing.

He does not expect his reader ever to fully understand it. Yet – if only in his fashion – he wants the book understood.

14 What is the meaning of a word? The gist of a phrase? The import of an episode? What is Joyce saying about Man? James Joyce? Ireland? Art or sin?

In the world of Earwicker – what is the age of his daughter? The religion of his wife? The day of his dream?

The naturalistic level is comparatively not important. It is a device, a tactic, that enables Joyce to speak of Man . . . of Joyce. . . . In another way, however, it's a central part of the design. In the system of the *Wake*, it is just a tiny star. But it is the star from which the much larger and important planets issue and around which they revolve.

To understand the book, no matter how imperfectly, we must first see it as a whole. To see it as a whole – no matter how imperfectly – we must acquire a sense of the little world of Earwicker. Here and there in the book, Joyce has hidden the material with which we may build it.

15 It is a week-end in Lent. The year is 1922.

There are indications in the text that confirm this period. But, when we have looked for signs that it's one day rather than another, we have not been so successful.

They should be there for the finding – I have looked for them again.

A would-be Holmes, I have sought a print, a scent, a twig that has been bent, a match that has been dropped. A word, a phrase, that has meaningfully been distorted.

16 In his opening Canto, Dante says the sun is in the Ram.

Joyce measures himself against Dante. He would be tempted, in his first pages, to make a similar statement. He might decide against it. But he would think of it.

On the first page, the second paragraph begins, 'Sir Tristram . . .' This contains the word 'ram'.

As a rule, the reader is too quick in announcing such a discovery. Each word in *Finnegans Wake* may have many meanings. That, however, is no franchise for opening the door to all of them. It is a

THE DATE OF EARWICKER'S DREAM 89

reason for being particularly cautious. Yet, in this case, the speculation is justified.

Joyce is almost as observant as his readers. He would have realized that it contains the 'Ram'. This is a theme that he was considering. He would not have suggested it—would not have come so close to it —unless he intended it.

The use of Tristram is an acknowledgement to Dante. It also has a place in the tension of the dream itself.

It is a first statement of Earwicker's fear.

This paragraph has seven principal clauses. They are a version of the Ages of Man. It begins with Tristram. Under different names, he moves through the clauses, getting older, weaker, till, in the last one, he comes to a 'rory end'.

The cycle starts again.

The son—Tristram—re-arrives!

He fears the son. He fears the day when his son will replace him. This is the equinox.

The time when the sun moves into the Ram.

17 'Not yet . . . not yet . . .' We are repeatedly told that the things in this paragraph have not yet happened.

The anticipation is worse than the realization.

Sir Tristram has 'passencore rearrived'.

We are not yet in the Ram.

The 18th of March is in Pisces. The 25th in the Ram. (In the time of Virgil, the 25th was the equinox. The Day of the Ram.) Thus, at first glance, an allusion to Tristram would seem to indicate that it's not the 18th.

But—as we saw—he has not yet re-arrived. We are still in Pisces.

It's the 18th of March.

18 Near the end of the book, there are many references to dying. No matter who is dying, in Earwicker's mind, the victim, on one level, is always Earwicker.

On p. 617, we read that a funeral will take place on 'toosday'. (In an early version, Joyce used a different day. But he thought it over. He put it on 'toosday'.)

How does this apply to Earwicker? Why is he buried twice? Today and Tuesday?

There is only one thing I can think of.

The dreamer fears the equinox. But, as we found—early in this essay, when discussing the equinox—this term is equivocal. In the spring, there are two times when the night is overtaken by day. The official equinox: the 21st of March. And the actual equinox, the actual day of parity.

If the dream starts on the 18th, 'today' is when he is going to have his funeral. His son is going to replace him. The 21st of March is on Tuesday.

We have a similar situation in September. On the 22nd, 'today' is the equinox. The day of parity is Tuesday.

Only it isn't autumn—it's the Lenten season. The 18th of March.

19 Shem is the side of Earwicker that most resembles Joyce. The side that is associated with the book and dream. Chapter Seven is the one that is devoted to Shem.

Shem is Hebrew for the Name. The life-giving Name of God. It is also James.

On p. 195—the end of this chapter—'He lifts the lifewand and the dumb speak.'

This is an echo of Luke xi, 14. 'Jesus was casting out a devil, and it was dumb. And it came to pass, when the devil was gone out, the dumb spake.'

Both of these quotations are descriptions of the artist. One shows the life-giving aspect. In the other—he exorcizes. In each—he gives a voice to what has been inarticulate.

When Shem (or Joyce) lifts his animating wand, there is an overtone of these verses from Luke. In his dream—and book—Joyce is casting out a devil.

20 On Sunday, in the Church of England and the Roman Catholic Church, there is a lesson—a reading of an excerpt from the Epistles and another from the Gospels. This quotation from Luke is the beginning of one of them.

Since the dream—starting Saturday—ends on a Sunday morning, there should be an allusion to its lesson.

Joyce may refer to a number of the excerpts. In quest of universality, he may even allude to all of them. However—this is the one that is given a special prominence.

It should be the one that is relevant.

In both Church of England and the Roman Catholic Church—it is a part of the lesson for Oculi Sunday.

The 19th of March.

Richard M Kain

'NOTHING ODD WILL DO LONG':
SOME THOUGHTS ON FINNEGANS WAKE
TWENTY-FIVE YEARS LATER

With *Finnegans Wake* on our hands we can ill afford to laugh at Dr Johnson's wrongheaded dogma that 'Nothing odd will do long', with its inapposite example, '*Tristram Shandy* did not last.' Sterne's novel was about seventeen years old when Johnson pronounced it dead; after twenty-five years, are we at a wake or an awakening? Even the quarter century which has elapsed seems not enough for the evaluation of Joyce's 'meanderthalltale', 'nonday diary', 'polyhedron of scripture'. A true understanding and appreciation requires no less than a revolution in sensibility, and, what is even more resistant to change, a thoroughgoing reorientation of linguistic expectations.

In discussing his work with Eugene Jolas, Joyce cited *Tristram Shandy*: '. . . I am trying to build many planes of narrative with a single esthetic purpose. . . . Did you ever read Laurence Sterne . . . ?' The multiple planes of *Finnegans Wake*, and its gigantic scope, were implicit in the last eight episodes of *Ulysses*, where the events in the foreground were almost smothered by extensive materials from embryology and literary history ('Oxen of the Sun'), abnormal psychology ('Circe'), or scientific data ('Ithaca'). In an unpublished letter of November 1923 Joyce suggested to Miss Weaver the need for a new critical term such as 'two plane', which would supersede the tag 'stream of consciousness'. *Ulysses* had been more than two-planed: indeed, as the author had explained to Carlo Linati in September 1920, *Ulysses* was 'an epic of two races (Israelite-Irish) and at the same time the cycle of the human body as well as a *storiella* of a day (life)'. And also 'a sort of encyclopedia', a transposed myth, a congeries of symbols. Similarly, the *Wake* was to be a book of the night, embodying, he told Edmond Jaloux, 'the esthetic of the dream, where the forms prolong and multiply themselves, where the visions pass from the trivial to the apocalyptic, where the brain uses the roots of vocables to make others from them which will be capable of naming its phantasms'.

Dream psychology was to be only the ground-plan of the *Wake*, as the stream of consciousness had been of *Ulysses*. Joyce's mind was always intent on seeking analogies, and his letters to Miss Weaver were filled with his discoveries of parallels from history and legend and a miscellany of languages. One paragraph (in a letter of 1 January 1925) brought in the Irish alphabet, Bruno, Tristan, Danish settlements in Ireland, the Venetian ceremony of marriage of the sea with its Viking parallel, and the languages Dano-Norwegian, Greek, German, Irish, Japanese, Italian, and even Assyrian, which he jokingly claimed to speak 'very fluently' and to own 'several nice volumes of it in the kitchen printed on jampots'.

Far from being merely the litter of an over-stocked mind, the accumulation of learning was to be marshalled for the purpose of creating a gigantic epiphany of mankind, an evocation of the Collective Unconscious as currently posited by Carl Jung. A good description of this idea is found in F. M. Cornford's *From Religion to Philosophy*, a book published in 1912, at about the time Jung was shaping his theory: 'the memory of a race, enshrined in a continuous tradition of myth, legend, poetry, retains knowledge. . . . The study of the unconscious contents of contemporary minds is bringing to light the fact–however it is to be explained–that people today, in their dreams, use the symbolism of the primitive, mythical themes such as rebirth, death, and resurrection, eating the god, and so on–symbolism that often coincides in surprising detail with the universal myths.'

Joyce knew Jung, of course, and he may have found the germ of his universal history in many other places. Regarding the views of Bruno and Vico, 'I would not pay overmuch attention to these theories, beyond using them for all they are worth', he suggested to Miss Weaver, 'but', and here is the significant and less well-known postscript, 'they have gradually forced themselves on me through circumstances of my own life' (21 May 1926). For, as we shall see, his method of working was selective, finding support for ideas which had already proved congenial, and weaving them into a tapestry of universal pertinence.

'NOTHING ODD WILL DO LONG' 93

It was a conception of staggering magnitude. It involved the undertaking of serious risks, necessitating as it did the exploitation of language to the utmost verge of unintelligibility. With prodigal abandon Joyce threw his energies into the task, accumulating bundles of notes, drafts and revisions, seemingly oblivious to the possibility of failure. 'I work as much as I can because these are not fragments but active elements and when they are more and a little older they will begin to fuse of themselves', he wrote to Miss Weaver in October 1923, almost echoing his words of July 1919 when in the midst of *Ulysses* he asserted that 'The elements needed will only fuse after a prolonged existence together.' In the mind of the author the sixteen-year effort was a matter of dedication. The book, like its predecessor, had to be written.

Yet Joyce was the first to have misgivings. Discussing the work in letters to Miss Harriet Weaver, he let his habitual mask of self-disparagement become a grimace; the tone was no longer mocking but despondent. He announced the first pages by citing an Italian adage, 'The wolf may lose his skin but not his vice' (11 March 1923). A few months later he referred to 'the *Earwicker* absurdity' (17 October 1923). As these citations from the letters are being made, there comes to hand Mr J. I. M. Stewart's recently published *Eight Modern Writers*. Mr Stewart interprets the *Wake* as 'the work of a man who has lived too much alone with his own daemon', the result being that 'Nothing Joyce wrote comes closer to a cry of pain.' And his chapter concludes with two haunting passages from the letters: 'Joyce recorded what is perhaps the final truth about *Finnegans Wake* in a letter to his devoted patroness, Harriet Weaver, written in 1926: "I know it is no more than a game, but it is a game that I have learned to play in my own way. Children may just as well play as not. The ogre will come in any case." And eight years later he wrote to the same correspondent: "Perhaps I shall survive and perhaps the raving madness I write will survive and perhaps it is very funny. One thing is sure, however. *Je suis bien triste*." '

Traces of Joyce's self-questioning remain in the text. The stifled cries arise from the pages: 'Was liffe worth leaving?' (230). Henry of Navarre's defection from Protestantism and Esau's archetypal role as dupe are linked in 'was Parish worth thette mess' (199). The portrait of Shem is penned with ill-concealed disgust.

It must be remembered that Joyce had had few serene moments during the sixteen years of gestation. His daughter's illness, the problems of censorship and piracy, his own eyesight—he said that he wrote 'like a person who is stunned' (17 December 1923), or, in facetious vein: 'Complications to right of me, complications to left of me, complex on the page before me, perplex in the pen beside me, duplex in the meandering eyes of me, stuplex on the face that reads me. And from time to time I lie back and listen to my hair growing white . . .' (16 November 1924). Both Miss Weaver and Ezra Pound were objecting to the new work. 'Do you not like anything I am writing', Joyce pleaded to his patroness. 'It is possible Pound is right but I cannot go back' (1 February 1927).

He could, however, consider an heir. Within a few months he broached to Miss Weaver the amazing idea of surrendering his pen to 'anyone who I thought had the patience and the wish and the power to write Part II' (12 May 1927). A week later he proposed James Stephens. On second thought the notion is not so preposterous as it sounds. Behind it lies the concept that language carries within itself its own momentum, at least in such a project as a universal history. The ground-plan was in hand, and the major thematic threads isolated. For the rest, it would be a matter of weaving and elaborating. No limit need be set to the elaboration, for when every item in a series has an infinitude of relationships with every other item and every other series, it matters little where one starts. The usual standards of relevance no longer apply. One of the basic linguistic 'axioms' listed by Mr J. S. Atherton, in *The Books at the Wake*, is that 'As words contain in themselves the image of the structure of the *Wake* they also contain the image of the structure of history. (Bruno.)' Far from being a crochet of the author, this idea is closely related to Joyce's other principles of history, theology, and ontology which Mr Atherton enumerates in his useful outline.

One is reminded of Mallarmé's exalted conception of the poet's great work, towards which creation itself moves: 'all earthly existence must ultimately be contained in a book'. The Book, 'The Orphic explication of the earth', will be 'a hymn, all harmony and joy; an immaculate grouping of universal relationships come together for some miraculous and glittering occasion'. Portentous as this sounds, literature was to Mallarmé essentially a game, '*le jeu littéraire par excellence*'.

Though weak eyesight precluded systematic scholarship, Joyce was an amateur of genius in traditional philology, the study of the interrelationships between language and culture. His natural bent and the circumstances of his life led him in this direction. We know of his constant curiosity about language, his musical ear, his sense of the poet's calling. To him words were from childhood not mere common coins of communication, but artefacts of beauty and significance, vital elements in human history, redolent with associations of people and places. His years of exile, happily at the intersections of European culture, intensified this interest. Trieste marked the confluence of Slavic, Greek, Latin and Teutonic elements. The Berlitz School provided an amusing as well as frustrating Babel. Zurich and Paris were to follow, and Joyce's associates and acquaintances represented many parts of the globe. In Paris he attended plays and moving pictures, no matter what the language and regardless of the condition of his eyes, letting the exotic syllables fall upon his ear and make their impress on his mind.

History as preserved in speech and as repeated in situation aroused his deepest response. Hence the delight he took in the speculative daring of Giambattista Vico and of Victor Bérard, both of whom shared Joyce's love of the poetry of history and the history of poetry. The double vision of the pastness of the present and the immediacy of the past induced a state of aloofness, which was the source of his bland indifference to contemporary tyranny. As one who saw in fascism or anti-semitism only another instance of perennial human folly he was seldom aroused to protest.

His preoccupation with permanence amid change made one sentence of Edgar Quinet a favorite, a statement which appears several times in the *Wake*: 'Today as in the time of Pliny and Columella the hyacinth disports in Wales, the periwinkle in Illyria, the daisy on the ruins in Numantia and while around them the cities have changed masters and names, while some have ceased to exist, while the civilizations have collided with each other and smashed, their peaceful generations have passed through the ages and have come up to us, fresh and laughing as on the days of battles.' Here is the informing principle behind the muted poetry of tree and stone, hill and river.

Though the works of man be doomed, amid the ruins there spring afresh not only hyacinth and daisy but the life of legend, preserved in language. Joyce's predecessor of the same name, Patrick Weston Joyce, opened a chapter in his popular work, *The Origin and History of Irish Names of Places* (which Joyce mentioned in 'Gas from a

Burner') with a comparison of topography and typography that anticipates the philological spirit of the *Wake*:

'The face of a country is a book, which, if it be deciphered correctly and read attentively, will unfold more than ever did the cuneiform inscriptions of Persia, or the hieroglyphics of Egypt. Not only are historical events, and the names of innumerable remarkable persons recorded, but the whole social life of our ancestors–their customs, their superstitions, their battles, their amusements, their religious fervour, and their crimes–are depicted in vivid and everlasting colours. The characters are often obscure, and the page defaced by time, but enough remains to repay with a rich reward the toil of the investigator. Let us hold up the scroll to the light, and decipher some of these interesting records.'

Interpreting the *Wake* is a vast archeological enterprise. Beginning slowly, with the *Exagmination* in 1929, it has proceeded at a gradually accelerating pace. Only within the last few years has the student been provided with much more than preliminary ground surveys and occasional assays in depth. Enough has been done to establish the wealth of the lode.

Recent views of the work by expert investigators raise the problem of whether the results are worth the effort. Mr Clive Hart, in *Structure and Motif in Finnegans Wake* (1962), judges that though 'potentially at any rate it is in the same class as *Ulysses*–which immediately puts it among the great books of the century', the question of 'whether the riches are sufficient to repay the considerable labour which must be expended' will 'very likely always remain a matter of taste and temperament' (30). In *Joyce* (1962) Mr S. L. Goldberg is more positive, asserting that 'I do not believe *Finnegans Wake* is worth detailed exegesis' (103). Mr J. I. M. Stewart, viewing the book largely as an exploration of the unconscious, believes that 'perhaps we can say only that a serious–or at least a brilliant–idea underlies the *Wake*; that the idea produced a certain limited success; that in the main however it proved not to work; and that something compulsive in Joyce obliged and enabled him to carry on, nevertheless' (468).

A writer of such magnitude induces an awesome respect, and it seems presumptuous of any critic to venture derogatory comment, no matter how hesitantly. Moreover, in the present state of our knowledge and awareness it would appear impossible to reach a verdict. Mr Atherton is probably most nearly correct in suggesting that 'a final literary evaluation' may never be made, since no complete understanding seems attainable. These reservations derive from the book's almost impenetrable obscurity. Obscurity can be, and has been, lessened, if not entirely eliminated.

A more insuperable objection remains. Save for moments of poetry and pathos, the author's farcical manner is seldom put aside. The constant japing resembles the forced efforts of a comedian who senses the loss of his audience and who resorts to the most obvious means of attracting attention. Life is reduced to a sequence of music-hall turns, comic routines with almost endless encores. Such strictures may be unjust, and perhaps with increasing acceptance of the punning mode this sense of distaste may diminish. Taken in small quantities, the joco-serious mode can be delightful, as audiences at recent dramatizations have discovered. *The Voice of Shem* and *The Coach with the Six Insides*, staged as fantasy, have been unexpectedly entertaining and successful on both sides of the Atlantic Ocean. The joy of life was projected in cascades of rollicking verbiage. The *Wake* still lives, though in a restricted milieu. On a more serious level, at least one reader feels that the explications of passages are often more interesting and more poetic than their expression in Joyce's text.

As an illustration of Joyce's stage-Irishry, one may note his distortions of the Quinet sentence quoted earlier. That this 'beautiful sentence' (22 November 1930) was loved by Joyce is apparent. He once astounded his protégé John Sullivan by reciting it as they walked along the Boulevard Edgar Quinet, and, as we have seen, its thought was congenial.

Mr Hart's elucidation of the Quinet motif is a brilliant tour de force which leads the reader through the involutions of Joyce's mind and the bypaths of history, numerology and other assorted topics. The expositor notes that much as Joyce may have admired the sentence, he was now 'long past the stage when he could comfortably write such simple stuff as this' and consequently he was forced to render the idea in elaborate dialect translations, for which 'parody' is the only approximate word we have, inadequate though it may be. 'The result is that all his reworkings inevitably annihilate Quinet's rather too self-conscious grace and delicacy' (188). True, but after the absorbingly interesting exposition is concluded, we return to the text of the *Wake* and find paragraphs of contrived distortion, a pennyworth of sack indeed.

These changes are sometimes informed by playful humor, wistfulness, or pathos, but too often they seem motivated largely by malice and mischief. Pliny and Columella in the Quinet sentence permute to 'plinnyflowers in Calomella's cool bowers' (354) and 'plinary indulgence makes collemullas' (319) to reach their final apotheosis in 'Plooney and Columcellas' (615). It is hardly too much to say that a great deal of this is less than rewarding.

Easier to discuss than to read, *Finnegans Wake* at present appears a vast, ineradicably flawed creation. Joyce's genius could breathe life into the most unpromising material, such as the statistical data in the penultimate chapter of *Ulysses*. Often when the reader feels that at last he has caught the author nodding, he is brought up short by some allusive obliquity which indicates that it was not Joyce's attention which was straying. The preternatural degree of involvement that Joyce demands is an earnest of his continuing fascination in the future. Like that curiously unsatisfactory and yet absorbing play *Exiles*, though to a far more profound extent, the *Wake* has its own unique compelling force. It does embody an original and significant world view, a multidimensional perspective. There it stands, an Everest of literature, a constant challenge to the courageous and the foolhardy.

In a confessional mood Joyce once exposed the bitter roots from which much of his later humor sprang. Parodying the beautiful conclusion of 'Anna Livia Plurabelle', he wrote to Miss Weaver in October 1928 that 'my ho head hawls and I feel as heavy as John McCormack but having some congenital imbecility in my character I must turn it off with a joke'. Considering the task upon which he was engaged, and the handicaps under which he labored, we may understand and regret the necessity.

A Walton Litz

USES OF THE FINNEGANS WAKE MANUSCRIPTS

The student of *Finnegans Wake* now has within his reach a detailed record of the work's complex development. Although the manuscript material in the British Museum is not complete for every episode, it does provide—in conjunction with the Buffalo workbooks and the published sections of *Work in Progress*—a massive challenge for the genetic critic. Already a significant portion of this material has been edited, and recourse to the manuscripts has become a standard tactic in criticism of *Finnegans Wake*.[1] This tendency will certainly continue. Probably most of us would casually agree with David Hayman's statement (in the Introduction to his *First-Draft Version of Finnegans Wake*) that the 'immense importance' of the *Finnegans Wake* manuscripts is 'self-evident', but in fact there seems to be no consensus as to why they are important or how they should be used. This confusion over methods and aims in the handling of genetic materials is not, of course, peculiar to Joyce studies. James Joyce's desire to make the growth of *Finnegans Wake* part of its subject-matter, and his willingness to expose the book as a 'Work in Progress', were merely extreme examples of that self-consciousness which has characterized so much European literature since the Romantic period. Given the rise of such an attitude, it was inevitable that interest in the creative process—and preservation of the by-products—would increase, yet this increase in interest and available evidence has not been accompanied by the necessary sophistication of critical theory and practice. Most discussions of the critical relevance of an author's drafts and revisions still turn on the problems of classical texts, or English texts of the seventeenth and eighteenth centuries, and they seem hardly adequate to guide the scholar through Henry James's complex revisions or the intricate evolution of *Finnegans Wake*.

The present essay does not pretend to 'solve' the problem of how or why an author's drafts and revisions should be considered. Any full rationale for the critical use of such materials would have to be part of a general theory of literary study, and could hardly make sense separated from that theory. What I have attempted is the identification of some possible uses for the *Wake* manuscripts, and a discussion of some limitations inherent in these uses. It is natural to believe that access to an artist's workshop will enhance our understanding of the finished product, but something more than faith is needed if we are to realize this goal.

Let us begin on relatively safe ground. As Fred Higginson and Clive Hart have shown, the published texts of *Finnegans Wake* are corrupt in many places.[2] Some of the changes made in typescript and proof never reached the printing stage; other errors were not noticed by Joyce when he prepared the *Corrections of Misprints*; and new mistakes were introduced when the *Corrections of Misprints* were incorporated into later editions. Of course, any editor must be cautious when he goes beyond Joyce's own corrections and emends from the manuscripts; Joyce's 'love of accidentals' is well known,[3] and some of the apparent errors may have received his silent sanction. But there is no reason why a good critical text of *Finnegans Wake* should not ultimately be produced, based upon judicious use of the manuscripts. Printer's errors are usually obvious, and other emendations can be tested in terms of local context. Mr Dalton's essay in the present collection shows how the text of *Finnegans Wake* can be improved through critical emendations and intelligent use of the manuscripts.

A second use for the early drafts and published fragments of *Work in Progress* lies in the charting of Joyce's artistic development. Without this evidence the seventeen years between the completion of *Ulysses* and the publication of *Finnegans Wake* would be mysterious indeed, and the foreshadowings of Joyce's later methods in the final chapters of *Ulysses* would seem much less obvious. One technique for tracing Joyce's development is to follow a single episode or passage from first to final draft.[4] But since Joyce's methods varied somewhat from episode to episode, and no single episode held his attention throughout the 1920s and 1930s, a selection of representative 'cross-sections' would appear to provide the truest record of changes in his art. Each critic will have his own notions as to which passages are most representative of Joyce's work at a particular point in time. My own view is that we should follow the conventions of textual scholarship, assuming that those sections which Joyce submitted for serial publication were more 'finished' than those left in manuscript, and that among the published versions those which terminate a continuous process of composition are most important. Thus the 1928 Crosby Gaige edition of *Anna Livia Plurabelle*, which culminated a five-year process of composition, would seem to reflect Joyce's current aims more fully than preliminary versions published simply as 'From Work in Progress'. The specific title, and commitment to book form, testify that it was Joyce's intention to present the public with an interim report on the development of his work, and suggest that he considered this particular episode as tentatively 'finished'. Of course, any principle of selection that is followed consistently will produce a fairly representative series of passages, but concentration upon the published fragments has the advantage of pointing up Joyce's conscious shifts in emphasis.

The rationale for studying *Work in Progress* at successive stages of its development seems clear and compelling, since such a study establishes the essential continuity of Joyce's artistic career. Much more complicated is the problem: how can an examination of the earlier versions aid in our critical appreciation of the final text? One extreme view of this general problem is neatly summarized by René Wellek and Austin Warren in their *Theory of Literature*:

'... if we examine drafts, rejections, exclusions, and cuts more soberly, we conclude them not, finally, necessary to an understanding of the finished work or to a judgment upon it. Their interest is that of any alternative, i.e., they may set into relief the qualities of the final text. But the same end may very well be achieved by devising for ourselves alternatives, whether or not they have actually passed through the author's mind. Keats' verses in the "Ode to the Nightingale":

The same [voice] that oft-times hath
Charm'd magic casements opening on the foam
Of perilous seas, in faery lands forlorn,

may gain something from our knowing that Keats considered "ruthless seas" and even "keelless seas". But the status of "ruthless" or "keelless", by chance preserved, does not essentially differ from "dangerous", "empty", "barren", "shipless", "cruel", or any other adjective the critic might invoke. They do not belong to the work of art; nor do these genetic questions dispense with the analysis and evaluation of the actual work.'[5]

In effect Wellek and Warren are declaring all previous states of a work to be mere indications of intention, as relevant or irrelevant to the final text as any other indication by the author of what he was 'trying to say'. This rigorous attitude (which can only survive in a *theory* of literature, and is here exaggerated by Wellek and Warren for cautionary purposes) is founded on the assumption that every change in a work of art, no matter how small, creates a new and totally independent work. Theoretically, this may be true; but in practice the critic has to distinguish between a more or less continuous process of composition and revisions made after a lapse of some time. The time factor, although imprecise, is crucial. Drafts which follow each other in quick succession are usually part of a continuous process in which related themes are extended and clarified, while changes made after a considerable lapse of time often go against the intent of the earlier work (as in Henry James's late revisions). There are, of course, many exceptions to this generalization (Yeats's radical shifts in direction within a brief period of time come to mind), but in the case of *Finnegans Wake* the connection between early and late versions is more intimate than Wellek and Warren will allow. The special nature of Joyce's language places the earlier versions in a special relationship to the finished work, and produces an extraordinary continuity in the process of composition. When Keats considered 'ruthless seas' and 'keelless seas' before settling upon 'perilous seas', he was exploring alternate avenues of expression. These alternatives do possess the status of having passed through Keats's mind, not that of the critic, yet the final version bears no necessary relationship to them; indeed, it may even contradict them. But Joyce's usual method was inclusive and expansive, not selective, a synthesis of common elements rather than a choice between alternatives. Thus when the word 'Listen' is altered to 'Essonne' during the rewriting of *Anna Livia Plurabelle*[6] (thereby introducing the Essonne river) the earlier meaning is gathered into the new compound, and examination of the earlier draft helps to confirm the nature of the portmanteau creation. Time after time in *Finnegans Wake* consultation of an earlier draft will suggest a nuance or extension of meaning which, once recognized, is obviously *there* in the finished work. Of course, it would be a mistake to attach great authority to these earlier drafts. The evidence of an early version is essentially *historical* (like the evidence of Joyce's reading or his personal experience): it shows that which is possible or probable, and stands in no absolute relationship to the finished work. But given Joyce's particular methods of word-synthesis and accumulated associations, the degree of probability in the relationship is quite high. In many cases the understanding of a passage in *Finnegans Wake* is virtually a re-enactment of the process of composition.

So the evidence of the manuscripts joins other historical evidence as an adjunct to interpretation, useful but not indispensable. Yet a glance at any study of *Finnegans Wake* which utilizes the manuscripts will show how difficult it is in practice to maintain this judicial attitude. The temptation to over-emphasize the critical importance of the manuscripts seems almost irresistible. The typical progress of a passage from simple to complex structure, from prosy statement to poetic language, seems to lead overwhelmingly to the assumption that the early drafts of *Finnegans Wake* are an authoritative *Skeleton Key*, the real source of the work's life. All our metaphors of growth—'root' ideas, 'skeleton' structure—imply that the meaning of the *Wake* can be discovered if, somehow, we can successfully trace the stream of composition to its source. In other words, the *Finnegans Wake* manuscripts pander to our love of paraphrase, and offer the tempting security of 'intentions': yet no work ever lost more through paraphrase than *Finnegans Wake*. Just as many of the leading ideas of the book seem flat and commonplace when stated, so do the early drafts seem flat in comparison with the texture of the finished work. How exciting to learn that a 'plain' version of Anna Livia's letter resides in the early manuscripts, and how dull to read it. Although many of us may insist that Joyce carried his methods of verbal elaboration beyond effective limits, there can be no doubt that the life of the *Wake* lies in this elaboration. Perhaps every critic of *Finnegans Wake* should be forced to re-read James's 'The Figure in the Carpet' before attacking the problem of the manuscripts.

To sum up this phase of my argument: the continuity of Joyce's work on *Finnegans Wake*, and the unique nature of the language he employed, place the successive drafts in a special relationship to the final text and render them of extraordinary use to the interpretative critic. But the evidence provided by the manuscripts is still subject to the limitations of all historical evidence. The finished work remains an independent creation, and its structure is the final arbiter.

Another important use of the *Finnegans Wake* manuscripts arises from what James S. Atherton has called the book's 'awareness of itself as a "work in progress" '.[7] Anyone reading the last chapters of Richard Ellmann's biography, or Joyce's letters of the 1920s and 1930s, soon realizes that during Joyce's later years the writing of *Finnegans Wake* became a major portion of his experience. Like all of Joyce's works, *Finnegans Wake* is on one level an autobiography, and his labors on *Work in Progress* join with Joyce's other experiences as part of the book's subject-matter. As Atherton has fully demonstrated, *Finnegans Wake* 'tells us a great deal about its own creation, and discusses its own manuscript at some length'.[8] Most of these references occur in section I, v ('The Hen'), which is just as much 'about' Joyce's struggle with *Work in Progress* as section I, vii ('Shem the Penman') is 'about' the better-known facts of Joyce's life. When viewed in this manner, the history of the *Wake*'s composition is seen as one more important area of information with which the intelligent reader should be familiar.

Finally, the drafts and revisions provide material for the biographer, and for anyone interested in Joyce's psychology or the nature of the creative process in general. The early fragments and workbooks – especially the *Scribbledehobble* workbook – point toward those shadowy regions where the subconscious origins of the *Wake* may lie, while the detailed expansions and revisions help to establish Joyce's habits of mind. All the general characteristics of Joyce's methods of composition – the exaggerated orderliness, the grotesque pedantry, the obstinate and avaricious hoarding of words and phrases – these fill in our picture of his mind, and are as much the subject-matter of biography as are the more obvious personal relationships. But the structure of an artist's life is not continuous with that of his art, and the Road to Xanadu is seldom the direct route to the poem. Here again future students of the manuscripts who are interested in Joyce's mind and the nature of the creative act cannot assume that the critical importance of their discoveries is self-evident.

Most of the caveats put forward in this essay have been directed at critics who would use the manuscripts as a basis for interpretation, but I believe they apply to editorial work as well. Perhaps it is possible to say that the editing of texts and manuscripts needs no defense. Perhaps future editors of the *Finnegans Wake* manuscripts will be content to rest on the modest justification that every scrap of an author's work should be easily available in accurate form. But even the most routine of editorial judgments often depend on interpretation, and given the complexity of his material the editor of Joyce's manuscripts can hardly avoid being a critic in disguise. So for editors as well as for declared critics the problems seem much the same. Any use of Joyce's drafts and revisions raises perplexing questions of literary theory, and the effectiveness of the critic or editor will depend in large measure on his willingness to face these questions and recognize the inherent limitations of any approach to the manuscripts.

NOTES

1 The *Finnegans Wake* Mss. in the British Museum (Add. Mss. 47471–88) are described in David Hayman's *A First-Draft Version of Finnegans Wake* (Austin, 1963), while my own *The Art of James Joyce* (London and New York, 1961) contains a brief catalogue of the Mss. and a chronology of the published fragments. See also John J. Slocum and Herbert Cahoon, *A Bibliography of James Joyce* (New Haven, 1953), pp. 99–101 and 145–8. Joyce's workbooks for *Finnegans Wake* are described in Peter Spielberg's catalogue, *James Joyce's Manuscripts and Letters at the University of Buffalo* (Buffalo, 1962), VI, A–D. The largest and most important of these workbooks has recently been published as *Scribbledehobble: The Ur-Workbook for 'Finnegans Wake'*, ed. Thomas E. Connolly (Evanston, 1961); Mr Jack P. Dalton is now engaged in the important task of editing for publication all sixty-six Buffalo workbooks. In addition to Hayman's *First-Draft Version of Finnegans Wake*, which presents with annotations the earliest versions of each episode, Fred H. Higginson has edited the entire development of a single episode in his *Anna Livia Plurabelle: The Making of a Chapter* (Minneapolis, 1960). Important manuscript fragments are transcribed and discussed in M. J. C. Hodgart's 'The Earliest Sections of *Finnegans Wake*' (*James Joyce Review*, I, February 1957, 3–18) and Fred H. Higginson's 'Two Letters from Dame Anna Earwicker' (*Critique*, I, Summer 1957, 3–14)

In recent years several commentators, notably Clive Hart (*Structure and Motif in Finnegans Wake*, London, 1962) and James S. Atherton (*The Books at the Wake*, London, 1959), have put their knowledge of the manuscripts to critical use. My own *Art of James Joyce* is partly devoted to a critical evaluation of the *Ulysses* and *Finnegans Wake* manuscripts, and the present essay may be viewed as an exercise in self-criticism

2 In 1956 Fred H. Higginson published a list of emendations based upon a collation of the printed sections of *Work in Progress* (*Journal of English and Germanic Philology*, LV, July 1956, 451–6). In a later issue of the same journal (LIX, April 1960, 229–39) Clive Hart drew upon his collation of the manuscript drafts to correct and amplify Higginson's findings. See also Hart's discussion of the text of *Finnegans Wake* in the Introduction to his *Concordance* (Minneapolis, 1963). Joyce's corrected copy of the *Wake* and his list of errata

(published as *Corrections of Misprints in Finnegans Wake*) are now in the Buffalo collection (Spielberg, VI. H. 4)

3 '[Samuel] Beckett was taking dictation from Joyce for *Finnegans Wake*; there was a knock on the door and Joyce said, "Come in." Beckett, who hadn't heard the knock, by mistake wrote down "Come in" as part of the dictated text. Afterwards he read it back to Joyce who said, "What's that 'Come in'?" "That's what you dictated," Beckett replied. Joyce thought for a moment, realizing that Beckett hadn't heard the knock; then he said, "Let it stand." The very fact that the misunderstanding had occurred in actuality gave it prestige for Joyce' (Richard Ellmann, 'The Backgrounds of *Ulysses*', *Kenyon Review*, XVI, Summer 1954, 359–60)

4 See, for example, my own comments on the evolution of the *Anna Livia Plurabelle* episode (*FW*, I, viii) in *The Art of James Joyce*, chap. III

5 *Theory of Literature* (New York, 1949), p. 86

6 On the *transition* proofs. See Higginson, *Anna Livia Plurabelle: The Making of a Chapter*, p. 64

7 *The Books at the Wake*, p. 59. The first chapter of Atherton's study contains a comprehensive treatment of the problem discussed in this paragraph

8 *Ibid*, p. 61

David Hayman

'SCRIBBLEDEHOBBLES' AND HOW THEY GREW: A TURNING POINT IN THE DEVELOPMENT OF A CHAPTER

Though he revised heavily and constantly added to his mosaic-like passages, Joyce was remarkably economical; he seldom discarded anything he had written and revised. Consequently, the three passages which he did feel obliged to abandon, or to refashion, merit close attention: the extension to the fair copy of 'Tristan and Isolde' which was to provide a setting for the poem 'Nightpiece';[1] the short account of Shaun delivering the letter to HCE found with the early drafts of Chapter I, v;[2] and the puzzling abortive passage from Chapter II, ii which Joyce intended as an introduction for 'The Muddest Thick'.[3] The first two of these passages were discarded after what amounted to a single revision, but for each of them Joyce later found other uses. Details like the handkerchief incident and the star imagery of Chapter III, ii were first exploited in the abandoned extension to 'Tristan'. The 'delivery of the letter' grew into Book III soon after Joyce finished drafting the bulk of Book I. But II, ii's abortive passage, which in its earliest version begins 'Scribbledehobbles are ...', has an infinitely more provocative and perplexing history. Whereas the other passages were written quickly, almost off the top of the author's head, this piece was the product of much preparation and thought. It was painfully elaborated in 1932 from extensive notes which appear to have been taken six years earlier in the *Scribbledehobble*[4] notebook, but Joyce saw fit after six revise-and-complete drafts to chop it into kindling, preserving intact only the first page or so, discarding a large segment and using most of the remainder in Issy's footnotes. This passage, which was to have been his introduction to the chapter as well as to the geometry lesson, became little more than an interlude when Joyce wrote the 'Storiella As She Is Syung' opening. Significantly, though he was at pains to publish the rest of the chapter, he never attempted to publish separately the rewritten central pages (*FW*, 275/3–282/4).

In the following essay I have attempted to give a detailed but necessarily provisional account of the genesis of these pages as they relate to Joyce's changing vision of the structure of II, ii.

By 1926, Joyce had in a manner of speaking nearly written himself out. He had composed and revised all of those sections of the *Wake* which grew naturally out of the early preparations and the vicissitudes of composition. Book III, the delivery of the letter to HCE, with its uninhibited narrative sweep, its brilliant exposure of the Shaunish mentality, had given him little trouble. Of Book I, with its unimpeded intellectual development, all but two chapters were written. The latter (I, i and I, vi) were added in 1926–7 to satisfy Joyce's conception of structure and his strict sense of balance and proportion and to provide the reader with the necessary synoptic view of theme, motif and character. There had been problems to face along the way: Chapter I, v, which introduced the female as opposed to the male vision, provided a turning point, forcing Joyce to reconsider earlier plans. The question of the ambiguous shift in the dream perspective had to be faced when he wrote III, iv. But from 1926 on his problems were far more complex. Somehow the substance of the book had to be concentrated in the central chapters which in accordance with his plans, no matter how sketchy they were at this point, were to treat the central or classical phase of the human experience. A more complex structure and a more subtle handling of materials were indicated. Joyce's letters of this period reflect a concern which he would probably have preferred to conceal.

Nevertheless, 1926 was a productive year. In the spring he was able to write most of the Catechistic chapter (I, vi) drawing upon previously-established character patterns and rhythms.[5] In the fall, using the ballad of 'Finnegan's Wake' as his armature and taking inspiration from notes pencilled in the back of his *Scribbledehobble* notebook, he wove his themes and motifs into an overture for the *Wake* (I, i). Meanwhile, during the summer, having put off the writing of 'question 11' for I, vi, he devoted himself to the mapping out of Book II and wrote down at least four separate though not quite distinct plans.[6] Most of the summer was taken up with the composition and revision of the geometry lesson which Joyce eventually named 'The Muddest Thick That Was Ever Heard Dump'

(*FW*, 286–304), but Joyce may also have found time to compose the extensive body of pencilled notes found on pp. 5–53 of the *Scribbledehobble*.⁷ It was from these notes, which bear so heavily upon problems of adolescence and the learning experience, that Joyce composed 'Scribbledehobbles are . . .' in 1932 or 1933. It seems logical that once he had finished drafting 'The Muddest Thick' Joyce should have started work on an introduction which would furnish that dramatic sequence with an adequate setting. To judge from later developments, the job was distasteful, and Joyce, whose spirits were none too high at the time, preferred to postpone composing the transitional passage, turning instead to the more rewarding job of composing I, i. Though he had already carefully outlined II, i, Joyce had only the vaguest notion in 1926 concerning the structure of Book II's lessons chapter. In addition to the notes he had nothing more concrete than the phrase from the early outline: 'Studies ⪥'.⁸

For reasons, some of which were doubtless physical, some emotional, Joyce made no effort to complete the composition of Book II before 1930 when he began to fill in the outline of II, i. In the meantime he considered passing the job of completing the *Wake* on to his friend James Stephens, who possessed the magical combination of attributes fitting him to be a successor. Joyce found little pleasure in writing II, i. His early drafts reflect a desire to minimize revision, to be relieved at least of that burden. His letters, though dispirited, are full of a curious semi-stoical pride: 'I enclose the final sheet of the first draft of about two thirds of the first section of Part II (2,200 words) which came out like drops of blood. . . . I think the piece I sent you is the gayest and lightest thing I have done in spite of the circumstances. . . .'⁹

Three months later he was still at work on his 'first' draft: 'I am also trying to conclude section I of Part II but such an amount of reading seems to be necessary before my old flying machine grumbles up into the air. Personally the only thing that encourages me is my belief that what I have written up to the present is a good deal better than any other first draft I made.'¹⁰

It is clear from the manuscripts that even before he had completed II, i, Joyce began work on 'Scribbledehobbles are . . .' and that he completed six drafts of that piece before he was able to finish drafting the earlier chapter. We note that the 'Storiella' opening for II, ii and the letter passages that were substituted for rejected portions of the abortive piece were written piecemeal in the same manner and with the same materials used by Joyce when he completed II, i.[11] Returning to his *Scribbledehobble* notebook he began to write an introduction for 'The Muddest Thick', drawing systematically upon each of the first fourteen pages of his notes, revising only slightly but adding heavily from the notes as he went. Of the 266 words in the completed first draft approximately 132 can be traced directly to the notes. The process continued when Joyce recopied and expanded his draft. Eventually he incorporated more than 75 of his *Scribbledehobble* entries in the first two drafts. Whether or not the notes were written explicitly for inclusion in Chapter II, ii, this was the first time Joyce made use of them. It is the only time (with the possible exception of his work on Chapter I, i in 1926 when he made similar use of the other set of pencilled notes) that he found it possible to use *Scribbledehobble* materials as a base for a complex and crucial passage. The extent of his dependence on these notes will be evident from the following version of the first draft. The starred words became 'annual' and 'marry' in later drafts. The italicized words were derived from the notes listed below.

'*Scribbledehobbles* are bent on their pensums *reading nails* & biting lips. *Trifid tongue others woo & work for* the *backslapper gladhander* and *dove without gall* and she whose *mind's a jackdaw's nest tearing up letters she never wrote* to solve *dulcarnon's twohornedheaded* dilemma what stumped bold *Alexander* and drove him *to pulfer turnips*. But, *my hat*, what a world of weariness is theirs *waiting to hear their own mistakes! For how many* guldens *would one walk now to* the pillar? For one hundred? For one hundred's thousand? And to what will't all serve them in an after *reeraw* world. Will it make of one a *good milker* having been *brought up on superlatives*? Will he *go away* in a *peajacket and not be silly*? Or where will he find funds to *smoke a whole box of matches* per day? Or if *she makes an earth of heaven* will she *lilt Barney take me home again*? As long as Una *reads serials in a bummeltrain with a lot of unexciting trousers about* it is *wholly probable that the holy parable* the worst at last at least may happen, such as *go to meet Mary, miss Mamy & mary* Meg*. Why ask her or *Tossy Madden* sense from what she's read since every *annal** has its own aroma? *Quid vobis videtur*?[12] And even the remembering a *tree is too beautiful for her to listen*. Small blame to her then if *she shook her shoe off at* geography class, doing rivers of India with *a whisper* of wilfulove *heard round the world*.'[13]

'SCRIBBLEDEHOBBLES' AND HOW THEY GREW   111

The following, listed in the order of their appearance in the passage, are the original notes from which Joyce made his draft.[14] He wrote the passage straight through to the end turning the notebook pages as he wrote. When he happened upon a note which fitted an earlier part of his draft, he made his additions without interrupting the composition process and without pausing to search further for new material to add. Thus the notes drawn from pages 13 and 14 represent the first steps in the revision of the completed text. The process was continued as Joyce revised his fair copy for Draft 2.

1. 'scribbledehobble'
8. 'T [Tristan] reads his nails'
2. 'trut trifid tongue' (Joyce probably crossed out 'trut' before he wrote 'trifid tongue'.)
13. 'others work or woo for T'
14. 'backslapper gladhander'
2. 'S P [Saint Patrick] dove without gall'
12–13. 'Kathleen's mind a jackdaw's nest'
13. ' ⊣ [Issy] tears up letters others work or woo for T' (Joyce made this note do double duty.)
3. 'dulcarnon=2 horned, 47th prop of Euclid or Alexander's 2 horn heads'
6. 'my hat'
3. 'to pulfer turnips'
12. ' ⊏ [Shem] listens to hear his own mistakes'
4. 'for how much would you walk to Barcola'
6. 'reeraw'
4. 'good milker' (preceded by 'Florrie is the only girl I love')
8. 'brought up on superlatives'
5. 'go away & don't be silly'
6. 'peajacket'
6. 'smokes a whole box of matches'
6. 'Irish colleen in heaven sings Barney, take me home again'
7. 'read serial in tram'
8. ' ∧ [Shaun] a lot of unexciting trousers' (followed by 'that's all I've got to say')
8. 'wholly probable (holy parable)'
8. 'go to meet girl meet other man' (last word may be 'marry')
9. 'Tossy Madden'
9. 'annuals (flowers)'

10. 'quid vobis videtur extra omnes'
11. 'L [Issy] trees too beautiful for her to listen'[15]
12. 'L takes off shoes at her(?) dinner'
12. 'T's whisper heard in Pekin'

It is obvious from the above that in writing this passage Joyce was very selective, using only a fraction of the available material, and that he assembled rather than composed, taking few liberties with the notes for which he furnished only the barest context. Considering the richness and variety of the notes from which Joyce made his choices, it is not surprising that he returned to them, but it is curious that he felt impelled to draw so heavily upon them for a passage which might after all have been written, in first draft at least, almost without recourse to notes. Why did he choose to hammer his raw material into a useful object practically without the intervention of the creative imagination? The probable answer is that he was not interested in this passage though he felt obliged to complete the lessons chapter. Perhaps also, after writing a long and lengthening first chapter for Book II, he felt more than ever the need in Chapter II, ii for something bulkier than 'The Muddest Thick' could ever hope to be in order to balance his structure.

It is likely that he failed to write the introduction in 1926 because he dreaded the drudgery of putting together a mechanical passage designed to introduce a chapter which was already in a sense complete, its function having been fulfilled by 'The Muddest Thick'. But it is also possible that already at that time he was searching for something more than a mechanical introduction, something to set off and balance the brilliant geometry sequence. Though it was bolstered in later drafts by the addition of a new opening relating the parents to their offspring, by the further addition of a paragraph disclosing the significance of the evening hour, and by a concluding paragraph dealing with the ritual and archetypal identities of the boys, 'Scribbledehobbles are . . .' remained a non-dramatic description of the children engaged in timeless chores, preparing for a future which is already in the cards.

Some time, probably late in the composition-revision process, Joyce hit upon the idea of the textbook format.[16] Accordingly, he had the typist leave generous margins on the final typescript and carbon of the abortive piece (Drafts 6 and 7). But even before this his interest in the passage had ceased to be perfunctory. The later drafts reflect less dependence upon notes and more on the familiar themes and motifs. The material was beginning to suggest new subject matter, fresh approaches.

These factors combined to bring about further developments. Joyce began by revising the carbon (Draft 6) intending to incorporate his changes in the typescript (Draft 7). Though they are not heavy, his revisions are significant. They reflect a continued interest in the passage and help mark the point where that interest began to flag. For when it came time to transfer the first few additions to Draft 7, he was deeply involved with the footnotes which he conceived of as an expression of Issy's views. Neither process advanced far. The footnotes and revisions, copied in a neat ink hand, stop after the first page of the typescript which also contains a handful of new revisions.[17] It would appear that when he began to compose the footnotes, he decided that instead of elaborating upon the draft, he would condense it. Accordingly, he drew the footnotes for page one of the typescript from other parts of the abortive section, especially from those relating to Issy. In effect he was reverting to an earlier stage of composition when he wrote notes like: '²My globe goes gaddy at geography giggle pending which time I was looking for my shoe all through Arabia' (*FW*, 275). To compose this note he had to pillage one of Issy's best sentences:[18] 'Small blame be hers therefore that she shook her simply shoe off at geography giggle, doing provinces of Persia, when Pa let me go too's tonic sulphur was outsung with a whispered wilfulness heard fore you could whistle an Ave from Hazelizod round this giddying globe!' To improve upon his first version of the note Joyce substituted 'pending which time' for 'so no wonder'. He drew his new phrase from the opening sentence of the typescript's last paragraph;[19] a sentence dealing with ritual kingship thus contributed to a note dealing with Issy's frivolous behavior. The third note on *Finnegans Wake* p. 275 now reads '³It must be some bugbear in the gender especially when old which they all soon get to look.' The sentence is a paraphrase of Issy's closing sentence:[20] 'For singleness on purpose is all their gender's bugbear especially when old which they all soon get to look.' Joyce had begun to turn his draft into source material, turn it on itself in effect. As he did so he began to cross through the reapplied material in orange pencil. Eventually, he bled the abortive piece of much of its vital substance and rearranged, rewrote or discarded most of what was left in favor of a new sort of development which I shall describe later. Nowhere else in the manuscripts do we find such radical revision of a carefully elaborated passage or such a large amount of discarded material. By translating a semi-jocular descriptive sequence into a series of farcical asides, Joyce began the process which enabled him to unify the chapter's disparate styles and approaches. 'Scribbledehobbles are . . .' did not suffice to furnish raw materials for all of the footnotes, but it did provide for most of the central pages and it sparked the composition of the rest.

It seems likely that before he had made too much progress with his footnotes, perhaps even before he began writing them, Joyce made two important additions to the typescript (Draft 7). The first of these (added to Ms. 47478, p. 289) recalls the Prankquean episode from I, i, but it is also the description of a rite of passage and therefore appropriate to this chapter which mediates between childhood and maturity. In its most primitive form it reads:

'They have through stairladder and the corridor of the heart a many a merry of taproom tales: how the lady O'Malley, a queen of graces, to the screes of Ben Edar came, to Hoved's chalet entrance, would night there but was denied, being unknown, so stole its heir, and went and came, again unknown, to earl changelord's hall but found it ever closed to her but her third veering, when she sent in her cowriecard, Annetta Little, Pranksomepark, let an imp into the lime of the lawrences and planted the enjamblement of the castlegrounds under the head in the faculty of tedious chaos and sunpromeners. Where an her hantle courts enticing Amy may lose a pleat or so.'[21]

The action of this piece was converted into that of the Norwegian Captain's tale told by the pub-clients in the setting evoked here. The 'corridor' was used in the description of Kate-the-slop's entry in Chapter II, iii, but it had previously been used in the description of the parent's moving to and from the twin's room in Chapter III, iv. I would suggest that Joyce used it again shortly after he composed the passage I have quoted, when he wrote the Cabalistic passage for the 'Storiella As She Is Syung' opening for II, ii: 'Easy, calm your haste! Approach to lead our passage!' (*FW*, 262/1–2). The key phrase in this case is 'corridor of the heart', which recalls the *Book of the Dead* and equates the pub-room-castle-home with the tomb or underworld and the pub-tales and drinking with the joys of the afterlife and the attained good.

Even more crucial, and probably even earlier, is the following short pencilled extension to the carbon (Draft 6), a description of primitive strife, flirtation and courtship: 'Till wranglers for wringawrowdy ready are and ere commences the commencement lead us seek, O jenny of eves the frivolest, who fleest from the fan but wouldst attach thee to thy thick eschewer.'[22]

It is hard to say when, but at some point early in the revision of Draft 7 Joyce must have seen in this sentence the way out of an impasse. It is then that he turned to the new opening, composing it piecemeal with the 'wranglers' paragraph as a nucleus. Later still he added the 'rite of passage' opening, the source of which I have described above. This sequence (*FW*, 260–6) in its turn suggested the new conclusion for the chapter as a whole. The fresh introduction, which took shape gradually in Joyce's mind and on paper, added cosmic dimensions and the sense of place, made the subject matter of the studies that much more vital. In effect Joyce rewrote for the 'Storiella' the heart of the 'Scribbledehobbles are . . .' identifying the boys with their history lesson and projecting a vision of Issy learning the grammar of seduction while belowstairs the parents are serving out the water of 'life' to the clients.

It may have been this development, the evolution of a new and better opening sequence, which decided Joyce to complete the dismemberment of the abortive piece. However, the chronology at this point is hard to establish. We can only judge from the results. At some point in the revision of the typescript and carbon (Drafts 6 and 7) Joyce, having become dissatisfied with the much-revised 'Scribbledehobbles are . . .', began using it as a source for his footnotes and decided to construct a new opening for the chapter. The rearrangement of the studies materials left a vacuum at the center of the chapter which Joyce filled piecemeal, probably after he had rewritten the opening paragraphs of 'Scribbledehobbles are . . .' and composed a large number of the footnotes and marginalia. As they now stand, the central pages (*FW*, 275–82) open with a glimpse of the parents tending to the clients while the children study upstairs. The two circumstances are linked spacially and temporally and to time and space by the sentences: 'Spell me the chimes. They are tales all tolled. Today is well thine but where's may tomorrow be' (*FW*, 275/24–6). These problems become more immediate when we zero in on the children and the present takes over from the past in preparation for the future which is being enacted belowstairs at this very moment. From the study room we shift to an evocation of the immemorial evening scene outside of the pub (*FW*, 276/11–

278/3). Then, returning to the students we focus on Issy who is training herself to write the letter of ALP by composing copy-book letters in the body of the text and an extravagant bit of juvenile seductive prose in a long footnote. These pages melt smoothly into a pastoral vision, a replay of the Quinet passage with commentary linking it to the brothers and Issy as aspects of history. In this radically altered version of the central pages Issy's role is preponderant. By discarding, playing down or rearranging the male-oriented passages (the discussion of the math and geometry problems and the boys' attitudes toward their studies) Joyce set Issy's behavior up as a foil for the boys' struggles with Euclid's first theorem and the mysteries of mature sexuality. It is in the order of things that her sexual awakening should precede and balance theirs. In addition, the Issy footnotes contribute throughout to impose her personality upon the male world of the studies, to introduce, that is, the irrational as a force in that world.

The development of the new Issy orientation for 'Scribbledehobbles are . . .' was probably as important an event in the history of II, ii as the composition of the 'Here . . . till wranglers' and the Grace O'Malley-Prankquean additions to Drafts 6 and 7. In all likelihood these events are interrelated. Doubtless Joyce conceived the letter-writing sequence when, while leafing through the pencilled notes at the end of the *Scribbledehobble* notebook in search of new material for his late drafts of 'Scribbledehobbles are . . .'[23] he came upon several pages dealing with the juvenile letter. It is no coincidence that the two types of letters found on these pages approximate the two types of letters he wrote for II, ii and that on one of these pages we read ' ⊢ [Issy] writes letter',[24] and on another a reference to Grace O'Malley.[25] But it is interesting that Joyce used none of this material directly in his drafts. The two missives, the primer letter (now *FW*, 280) and the juvenile seduction letter (*FW*, 279, n.1) were both designed for inclusion in the body of the text. There is no mention of the footnote until Joyce's second typescript of the seduction letter, which was first written piecemeal and then numbered and assembled. Set off from the text as a footnote the letter became a foil for the long Shem parenthesis in 'The Muddest Thick', adding one more element of balance to complete the structure of the chapter and resolve the difficulties raised seven years earlier by the composition of the geometry lesson.

In some of its details this account of II, ii's genesis is doubtless open to question. The whole story has yet to be told, but I believe that in 1932 Joyce, being in a none-too-creative state of mind, turned to a chore he had put off for seven years, looked for the easiest possible solution to the difficult problem of structuring an important chapter. The process of writing and revision with the aid of the *Scribbledehobble* notes brought with it needed inspiration and perhaps enthusiasm. As a result he was able, among other things, to conceive the textbook format, develop the 'Storiella' and through the dismemberment and reconstitution of the central pages highlight Issy's role as a female force.

NOTES

1 *A First-Draft Version of Finnegans Wake*, edited by David Hayman (Austin, Texas, 1963), pp. 210/2-211/26
2 *Ibid*, pp. 90-1
3 *Ibid*, pp. 148-55
4 Edited by Thomas E. Connolly (Evanston, 1961), pp. 5-53
5 See my account of this chapter in *A First-Draft Version*, p. 27
6 See *Letters*, pp. 241, 242 (21 May, 7 June and 15 July) and *A First-Draft Version*, plate I. The last item is the cryptic but detailed outline included in the notebook in which Joyce wrote early drafts of III, iv, 'The Muddest Thick' and I, i. James Atherton (in 'Finnegans Wake: The Gist of the Pantomime') has mistakenly identified it as the plan of Book III which was written long before Joyce began work on the material in this notebook
7 The dating of these notes is problematical since I can find none which Joyce used before 1932. Mr Connolly wrongly attributes some of those used in II, ii to other chapters but his correct attributions will serve as a handy index. Those he lists from Book I, chapters iii, iv and vi (not all of them are correct) were added to the *Transition* pages which Joyce revised in 1936 for the printers of *Finnegans Wake*. Those used in II, i and ii date from 1932 or later. Only the Book II notes were used in primary drafts
8 See plate I of *A First-Draft Version*
9 *Letters*, 22 November 1930
10 *Ibid*, 16 February 1931
11 This fact also accounts for the presence of notes from the *Scribbledehobble* in the late sections of the children-at-play chapter. It should be made clear that nowhere in II, i did Joyce use the pencilled notes to build extensive passages, though there are important clusters of notes on pp. 244, 247, 252, 254-5 and elsewhere. I mention this in order to emphasize the peculiarities of the abortive piece
12 Italicized in Joyce's text but also derived from the notes
13 *A First-Draft Version*, p. 148
14 In a few instances I have altered the note as reproduced in the published

version of the *Scribbledehobble* to correspond with the original. Though all of these notes were crossed through in red, I should mention that two of those used in Draft 2 were not crossed out. The numbers preceding the notes refer to Joyce's numbering of pages in the *Scribbledehobble*

15 The three positions of the T which stand for Issy in the notebook may well represent three aspects of the girl-woman. She is also called I and Is in the notebook. I would suggest that ⊥ is the most childish of the three and that ⊢ is the most mature

16 There is no evidence that he had considered the idea earlier, but there is no way of placing the moment of decision either

17 Later Joyce added marginalia for *Finnegans Wake*, pp. 275, 281 and 282. Apparently the footnotes had priority

18 *A First-Draft Version*, p. 153/38 ff.

19 *Ibid*, p. 154/22 ff.

20 *Ibid*, p. 154/20–1

21 *Ibid*, p. 151/n.43

22 *Ibid*, p. 142; an unrevised version of *FW*, 266/20–30

23 In late drafts of 'Scribbledehobbles are . . .' Joyce used notes from pp. 746, 750 and 762 (*Scribbledehobble*, pp. 129, 133, 145). At about the same time he was looking for additions for II, i

24 Misread by Mr Connolly as 'twister letter'

25 '. . . Grazia O'Mavrey (?) with all her gracies . . .' *Scribbledehobble*, p. 139. Cf. the reference to 'lady O'Malley, a queen of graces' in the Grace O'Malley passage added to Draft 7 and cited above

Jack P Dalton

ADVERTISEMENT FOR THE RESTORATION

In July of 1923 Joyce finished as the third fragment of his new work a hagiographic account of St Kevin. Having dictated to Nora the simple fable, he set to the work of elaboration much like an ancient illuminator and soon brought it to the state which appears, with minor revisions, at 605.4–606.12. Most of the elaboration was based on the mystic numbers 7 and 9. Kevin journeys to the supreme center of nine concentric circles (left to the reader) to prepare his baptismal bath by activities in sevens (605.26, 29, 30, 32). His soul ascends by nine levels–'poor Kevin',[1] 'piously Kevin',[2] 'holy Kevin', 'most holy Kevin', 'venerable Kevin', 'most venerable Kevin', 'blessed Kevin', 'most blessed Kevin', 'Saint Kevin'.[3] There are the nine orders of angels, the seven orders of clergy, the seven canonical hours, and the seven sacraments, each group in perfect order, except that, of the clergy, exorcist and lector exchange places, an alteration of no consequence. There are seven liturgical colors[4] and the seven gifts of the Holy Spirit.[5] The tub is named seven times (605.8, 14–15, 21, 32, 606.2 (bis), 7). The seven cardinal virtues are explicit in 'fortitude, acolyte of cardinal virtues', but they were best left out, as only three of them are Christian–a fact which did not however prevent a pagan virtue being the one named: at least fortitude is also one of the seven gifts of the Holy Spirit. Further sevens are implicit: Kevin was seven years old when sent by his parents to be educated by monks; his years of solitude at Glendalough were seven; the ecclesiastical establishment at Glendalough was noted for its Seven Churches; seven visits to Glendalough were equivalent to one pilgrimage to Rome. All of this, and much more, unfolds in one 431-word sentence of masterfully straightfaced comedy.[6]

Spatially the episode shows two superimposed crosses laid over the nine concentric circles. The first cross is made by angels and clergy–angels ascending, clergy descending.[7] (This neatly illustrates Lancelot Andrewes's dictum that the further one is from the Church the nearer to God. Thus it is with Kevin, who moves from death to life—see 605.3, where the reversal is explicit. On other levels his movement is to be understood differently.) This cross is joined at a spot just short of the center of the episode itself—'acolyte of cardinal virtues' (605.24–5):

angels	605.06		
archangels	–.11	priest	605.07
principalities	–.17	deacon	–.15
powers	–.18	subdeacon	–.21
virtues	–.25 ——	acolyte	–.24
dominations[8]	–.32	exorcist	–.36
thrones	606.03	lector	–.33
cherubim	–.06	doorkeeper	606.08
seraphim	–.10		

The first cross is one of Space, the second, one of Time. The canonical hours carry Kevin forward through the labors of his day/life, the sacraments backward. The sacraments are these: baptism, confirmation, the Eucharist, penance, extreme unction, holy orders, matrimony. The last two are special, not necessary to the Christian life, but the others are common to all (of certain rites) and arranged in order from birth to death. Joyce uses these five sacraments in time to complete the second cross. It is joined at a spot just past the center of the episode—'at sextnoon collected gregorian water sevenfold and with ambrosian eucharistic joy of heart . . .' (605.30–1):

matins with	605.09	matrimony	605.09
lauds	–.14	holy orders	–.15
prime	–.18	extreme unction	–.22
tierce	–.23	penance	–.23
sext[9]	–.30 ——	the Eucharist	–.31
nones	606.03	confirmation	–.35
vespers	–.04	baptism	606.11
compline	–.06		

In the center of the episode stands 'venerable Kevin' in the middle of his soul's perfecting. The regularity of the arrangements stops at a certain point, however, for intruding between 'venerable Kevin' and the center of the first cross is 'most holy Kevin'.

It is only poetic justice that there should be two cruces in the piece. The first is plain to anyone who tried to find dominations at 605.32: they are not there. For a number of years their absence exercised and overheated a number of scholars, who corresponded ingeniously on the matter. There is no place for the angels to be hiding, nor should they be, for the episode, despite its phenomenal complexity, is lucid and transparent in texture. After some study of angelology—a science new to me—the problem presented itself in terms of simple logic. The first proposition—without apologies—was this: the omission of the order was either deliberate or inadvertent.

If deliberate, why? There is no shortage of theories which can be, and have been, put forward, but none of the theories known to me—it is in this case safe to say, none of the theories possible—had any merit beyond the appeal of risible absurdity. In the hierarchy of angels which Joyce would be expected to follow and which he did follow (the most familiar, that of the Pseudo-Dionysius, followed by Aquinas and Dante in *Par.*, XXVIII, 99–126), dominations occupy no significant position, such as being the order in the center of the list, or so forth.

Inadvertence. It was clear that in this case the answer would be found, if at all, in the manuscripts, and that some help might be got there even if the omission had been deliberate. Anticipating use of the conventional hierarchy, the search was conducted between 'virtues' and 'enthroned'. The solution was thus immediately discovered, though its implications were several years in realizing themselves completely.

The drafts found on Buffalo Ms. VI. B. 3.42–5 and British Museum Add. Ms. 47488.24 have nothing relevant, but that on –.25 shows the following (original lineation, but omitting from the second line a crossed-out 'of' after 'domination'):

> water and with eucharistic joy of heart recedes carrying the
> lustral domination contained within his most portable
> privileged altar unacumque bath which severally seven times,

The next (–.25–6) reads (on –.26):

> joy of heart receded carrying that privileged
> altar unacumque bath which severally seven

Since the beginning of this draft follows the preceding on the same sheet, and taking into account textual considerations too lengthy to go into here, we can rule out the possibility of an intermediate draft.[10]

Now, Joyce was at this time recovering slowly from a serious bout of eye trouble, and his second fair copy (–.25) would have been difficult to read at the best of times: the hand is poor, the lines long and crowded close together. If there were a crossed-out 'the' replaced by 'that' we could be surer of what happened, but the change from 'recedes carrying the' to 'receded carrying that' is effected with no visible emendation. The shift of verb tense was deliberate and correct (in this draft Joyce put the entire latter part of the piece into past tense), and may have subtly called for 'that', which in turn leads more easily into 'privileged' than 'lustral'.

St Kevin was added to Book IV in 1938. The episode is on –.37–8; the missing line should have been on –.38. Along the left margin of –.37 Joyce wrote: 'This typescript is too faint. Can't read it.' This is strange, for my conclusion from the evidence is that –.37–8 were done at the same time as the rest of this third typescript and on the same machine. Mr George D. Painter of the British Museum has inspected the originals for me, concluding further that the same ribbon was used, the pages being the exact tint of those foregoing. Concerning the typescript as a whole, Mr Painter finds it not so much faint as showing the incipient greyish tinge which comes when the ribbon is just beginning to need replacement. Be this as it may–the psychological implications fascinate–if Joyce could forget dominations in 1923 there is slight chance that he would remember them more than fourteen years later.

Things such as these are evidence, but only corroborative. It is in the analysis of the episode itself that an answer must be found, and I think that after study reasonable men will be hard put reasonably to disagree. Joyce's known working methods, the draft history, and the materials, structure, and texture of the episode are such that, mindful of the cardinal fact that *exactly one line* was excised, even the most sober attempts at justification seem to me sophistical in the extreme. In fact, it must be considered that the primary effect of omitting the line was not to leave out an order of angels, but to wreck the syntax of the sentence. The verb 'effused' (605.34) cannot have 'altar *unacumque* bath' (–.32) as its object, for only a liquid can be effused. The container is effused *from*. This means that 'which' (–.32) stands with an impossible antecedent. In the first drafts the action is quite plain: the first reads, 'he goes to the brink of the pond and fills his tub with water which he emptys [Nora's sp.] time after time into a cavity of his hut', the second, 'venerable Kevin goes to the lakeside and fills time after time a tub with water which time after time most venerable Kevin empties into the cavity of his hut'. The 'lustral domination' of the next draft is the 'water' of these. 'Lustral' means 'of or pert. to, or used for, purification', and it is the purifying power of water, real and imagined, which is the basis of Kevin's activities. Note that at −.36–606.1 he 'exorcised his holy sister water, perpetually chaste'. Pure and purifying, it regenerates (606.10–12).[11]

The importance of syntax can hardly be exaggerated, but symbolism is also of great importance in *Finnegans Wake*, especially in a passage such as this one. Consider then that the primary effect of omitting an order of angels was not to leave the list incomplete and substitute an 8 for a 9, but to wreck the first cross, the one more symmetrical to begin with. A list of eight orders has no integral center, rendering a shambles the perfection of 'acolyte of cardinal virtues'.

What to do? Far too much is at stake to be overly concerned with 'that'. A time for action comes, and I briefly propose that *FW* 605.32 read: 'the lustral domination contained within his most portable privileged altar *unacumque* bath, which severally seven times'. The reader need not pass immediate judgment on this proposal, for we have yet to consider the second crux. It in fact comprehends most of the first and is simply stated: *The episode/sentence is a syntactic bog. It does not parse.* The reader will have more pleasure and profit from it if he will stop at this point and test the matter for himself. In any case, preliminary exposition is unnecessary here, the crux being established in its resolution:

1	605.25	delete comma after 'floor'
2	605.32	read as given above
3	605.34	delete comma after 'Kevin'
4	606.02	delete comma after 'handbathtub' (emended below)
5	606.03	delete comma after 'Kevin'
6	606.03	delete comma after 'enthroned'

The effect of item two on the sentence's syntax has already been fully considered and the fault laid to Joyce. Immediate blame for the rest of the mess lies with the third typescript,[12] a fine piece of work indeed. Though somewhat extreme, it is an example of what *Work in Progress* was up against and how Joyce responded. It typed 'apicentric' for 'epicentric', 'blassed' for 'blessed', 'inetconcentric' for 'interconcentric', 'center' for 'centre', 'az' for 'as' (the 'z' so light that the succeeding typist read simply 'a'), 'chirch' for 'church', and 'beptism' for 'baptism', lost off the side of the page the comma after 'fortitude', and omitted the 'at' after 'ubbidience'. Joyce noticed none of these mistakes until the final typescript, where five of the nine given here, a fraction over half, were dealt with, but the correction of 'inetconcentric', according to my analysis below, botched. In the surviving galley proof 'apicentric' and 'beptism' appear, as does 'center', which persisted into page proof (*v.* note 15), and the comma is missing after 'fortitude'. This half of the story is technically a comedy, since it comes out happily (except for 'inetconcentric'): the other half is not.

Joyce was unable to read the second typescript, finding it 'too faint', and had therefore entrusted some of the necessary revisions to the next typist. There are two notes; this is the second, written at the top of the page: 'Kevin and Glendalough[13] should have a capital initial all through this piece.[14] Also the piece should be punctuated properly.' Certainly it should have been punctuated properly, since even Joyce's own final fair copy had been typically less than perfect in this respect, but the typist's idea of how to accomplish the feat consisted of seeing that most of the 'Kevin's were set off by commas. Here is what happened to the syntax:

1. The introduction of a comma after 'floor' separated object from subject and verb. The typist had also introduced a companion comma after 'most holy Kevin', separating subject from verb, and this comma survived into galley proof. Joyce's attention was probably helped to the spot by the 'arinary' which had persisted from the second typescript, but more important must have been the fact that this comma fell at the end of a line, where punctuation is most conspicuous. A further comma had been introduced after 'holy Kevin' (605.22), separating subject from verb; it survived into galley proof, likewise fell at the end of a line, and was likewise deleted.

3. The introduction of a comma after 'most venerable Kevin' separated subject from verb.

4 and 5. The introduction of two commas to set off 'most blessed Kevin' separated, firstly, object from subject and verb, and, secondly, subject from verb. In galley proof Joyce noticed this situation but,

as with 'most holy Kevin' (item 1), did not take the time to understand it, for he

6. introduced a comma after 'enthroned', perfecting the disaster entirely. The past tense verb 'enthroned' was now a participial adjective referring to 'most blessed Kevin', which is to say, an essential had been transformed into a nonsensical ornament.

It must be said that my reconstruction of the mechanism in operation here might be false or at best a conflation, for there is one clue which could lend weight to the theoretical possibility of an intermediate typescript: between the two typescripts in question the word 'cocreated' became 'concreated'. This could have been a typist's slip, but it could have been a revision. For example, the typist copying the second typescript was unable to improve on the punctuation, forcing Joyce to take the matter in hand. He added various commas and changed 'cocreated', the typescript was redone, and discarded or lost. We can admit, then, the possibility of Joyce himself wrecking the syntax, thus tying the whole business into a Gordian knot. Someone may conjure Joyce 'the pervasive ironist' and declare the syntax wrecked on purpose, another may conjure Joyce the unconventional punctuator, a fabulous creature. I fail to see, though, how in the end this can detract from my posing and resolution of the crux. Merely to say 'Gordian knot' tells us what we may do with it. For warrant, if one were needed, Joyce's own note would suffice, and a more direct one it is difficult to imagine: 'Also the piece should be punctuated properly.' Right.

I discovered the existence of the second crux while attempting to deal fully with the first, and the examination of the manuscripts necessary to its resolution resulted in the isolation of other spots of corruption, emended as follows:

'Ysle' read 'ysle' (605.17): In autograph and first surviving typescript (on -.37) it appeared 'isle'. On -.37, the first page of this typescript, Joyce wrote two notes, one in the left margin and one at the top. The former has not been quoted in full, for after Joyce had alleged a faintness of the typescript and an inability to read it, he gave this instruction for revision: 'Please first change all initial 'i's to 'y's: e.g. ysle not isle'. Three he changed himself, the two in the first line ('ysland of Yreland') and the only occurrence of 'isle'/'ysle', the words mentioned in the note. The 'y' of 'ysle' is a bit large in relation to the type, and was taken as a capital by the succeeding typescript (on -.58). Its form is not that of a capital, however. It matches precisely the 'y' of 'ysland', both being written cursive with long tails below the line: the 'Y's of 'Yreland' and of 'Yad' and 'Yed', added by hand to this typescript, are printed. It was size in isolation which fooled the typist; the 'y' of 'ysland' was no smaller, but stood in marked contrast to the 'Y' of 'Yreland'. Analysis, therefore, gives us far more than enough assurance, and we may also admit Joyce's note in evidence: '. . . e.g. ysle not isle'.

'ubidience' read 'ubbidience' (605.29): In the second typescript 'ubbidience' was substituted by hand for 'obedience' (–.37). So it appears on –.67, but when this page was redone (–.59) the word met with an accident: all of its letters were typed, but the first two fell one on top of the other. The succeeding typescript (on –.83) picked it up as 'ubidience' and so it went to the printer.

'hanbathtub' read 'handbathtub' (606.2): Appeared 'handbathtub' in three autographs and three typescripts (in the first two drafts it was simply 'tub'). In the last typescript the 'd' was omitted (–.83) and so it went to the printer.

'concentric' read 'interconcentric' (606.3): Draft history: Buffalo –.44–5: 'in the middle of the pool'; B.M. –.24: 'in the centre of the pool'; –.25 and –.26: 'in the intercentre of the translated water'; –.27 and –.38 (typescript): 'in the interconcentric centre'. On the succeeding –.67 we read 'in the inetconcentric center',[15] faithfully preserved in the next typescript and into the next. Joyce looked closer at the typescript to be sent the printer and noted–he or someone, as the handwriting does not appear to be his–this among other things. 'inet-' seems to have been taken for a garbled 'the', for it was crossed out and a 'the' written above, a redundant 'the'. Both 'the's are circled, so it would appear that someone other than Joyce noticed the redundancy: had he himself noticed we should expect one to be marked out, not both circled. As a result of this confusion, an emphasis which he had thought desirable in the growing complexity of the episode is lost: the tub, counted, makes a tenth circle, whereas both Kevin and his tub are within the center of the nine concentric circles surrounding. Emended in no fewer than five particulars, this passage now shows a much different face to the world: '. . . which handbathtub most blessed Kevin ninthly enthroned in the interconcentric centre of the translated water . . .'

'Yee.' read 'Yed.' (606.12): As mentioned above, the vowel-change pair 'Yad.' and 'Yed.' was added fore and aft the second typescript. In the three succeeding typescripts 'Yed.' appeared

'Yed.', but in the galley proof (–.208) it became 'Yee.' This could have been the fault of either the compositor or the monotype machine, a complex and delicate mechanism, and for the sake of argument we can admit in theory the possibility of Joyce sending to the printer a communication, written or verbal, the possibility of a further typescript embodying the change, or the possibility of an earlier galley proof on which the change was made. Unless he is firmly grounded in the manuscripts and in *Finnegans Wake*, the reader may wish to reserve judgment. All considered, I cannot bring myself to doubt the emendation—Joyce's use of such pairs, and groups, of interlocking words is all but unique, if not unique, in the history of literature, and as note 6 pointed out, this episode is particularly rich in them—but the most important thing to establish for the present is this: if it is insisted that 'Yed.' cannot be proven, it must be admitted that neither can 'Yee.' In short, no rational man can deny at least a substantial possibility the change was casual. Whether or not the future explicator accepts the emendation, he must know he stands here on shaky ground and he must explicate accordingly.

'super' read '*super*' (605.15): Three other of the tub's names are of this nature: '*altare cum balneo*', 'bath *propter* altar', and 'altar *unacumque* bath'. Why do we not read 'altar *super* bath'? As background let us consider italicization in the autograph drafts. In the first there is none, and only the words 'Doctor solitarius' would require it. In the second we find '*doctor solitarius*', but the newly added tub names are entirely roman. This state was carried over to the next draft, into which were then inserted '*cappa magna*', but 'extempore'. In the final fair copy Joyce added the remaining italics which appear in *FW*. It is a study in itself to consider how many arguments can be adduced both pro and con, and in the end we must admit there is no final proof. The fact that Joyce was careless with punctuation and underlinings in his final fair copies does not demonstrate a carelessness here. We do not know when the italics were added, whether while writing or afterwards; in both cases a mistake could have been made, more easily perhaps in the latter. I myself cannot fault the immediate commonsense judgment which calls for '*super*'. I must add that I am not influenced by the fact that this gives us seven italicized items; I think it accidental.

'handbathtub' read 'hipbathtub' (606.7): As we have noted, the tub is named seven times. The first four names are of one definite pattern, the last three of another.[16] Let me begin at the beginning by saying that Joyce first thought of Kevin's tub as a hipbath. Shortly after the first draft we find 'S Kevin–hip bath' (Buffalo Ms. VI. B. 3.80) and on VI. B. 10.85 we find 'hip-bath (semicupio)'. He used one or the other note when writing 'hiptubbath' into the first fair copy at this point in the text. Elsewhere in the draft the tub was only a tub. Six other names were devised for the next fair copy; in the next, 'hiptubbath' became 'hipbathtub' and thus in the final fair copy we find 'tubbathaltar', 'handbathtub', and 'hipbathtub'. As we should expect, these names are not random, but form an orderly progression. The word 'altar', present in the first four names and trailing in the fifth, is dropped from the last two; what had begun as altar and served as boat and bucket was now to be used as semicupe: the tub, also, is involved in the ascending and descending movements in the episode. As Kevin handles the tub to place it in the middle of the pool it is a 'handbathtub'; as he immerses in it his loins it is a 'hipbathtub'. So far, so good, yet on the latter's appearance in typescript it has become a 'handbathtub'. There is nothing else in the way of a revision; we are to believe Joyce changed this one thing of all. Of the two typists involved, I think it was Miss Weaver who made the mistake. Her typescript does not survive, but we know that it was she who typed, for example, 'priune' for 'prime' and 'landing' for 'lauding'. The word 'hipbathtub' she found in a distinctive position in her copy: it began the verso. It looked like that other long word starting with 'h' which she had typed a moment ago. She repeated: 'handbathtub'. Within the context of what I know of the episode, the book, and the author, this emendation seems to me routine, but since it may startle others, it is best to resolve the matter into a more basic form, one in fact basic enough to cover almost all emendations of this text. To paraphrase Fredson Bowers,[17] it is surely better to reproduce in a definitive edition a few words that are actually Joyce's in their origin, even though not his final intentions, than it is in such an edition to foist on his text words that are not and never were Joyce's.

delete comma after 'Kevin' (606.4): 'Hydrophilus' was inserted between 'Kevin' and a comma on -.26, and on -.27 we read ', Saint Kevin Hydrophilus, '. On -.38 Joyce changed the 'u' to 'o', and on -.67, -.59, and -.83 we read ', Saint Kevin Hydrophilos, '. In galley proof (-.208) 'Kevin' fell at the end of a line, followed by a comma. It would require an essay to introduce the non-bibliographer to the subject of line-endings. Suffice it to say that it is very easy to dismiss this comma as an error in setting, and we must. First, all manuscripts and typescripts lack it. Second, it is clear that the name 'Saint Kevin Hydrophilos' is modelled on the type 'Saint John Chrysostomos'. We know, then, Joyce's first intention, and we understand it. On the other hand, we have no certain record of a different later intention, and we would not, I think, understand it if we had it. As part of the satisfaction we have in the line-ending a known cause of such errors. Thus, in deleting the comma we are following the only known valid intention of the author, and the odds overwhelmingly favor this course.

We have run up and down a gamut, and there is no denying that its upper end is at first disturbing. Nevertheless, it has seemed to me that the episode is in many ways an ideal classic passage to establish the necessity, desirability, and practicability of emending the text of *Finnegans Wake*. It is an atypical segment, and it cannot now be settled whether this has been for it or against it, or both, and to what degree(s). This is to say it may not be statistically reliable. It need not be, but if it is, there will be about 7,000 emendations to present. The figure is astounding, but, after all, it is only a very small fraction of the total number of characters in the book – by a rough calculation, well over 1,100,000. In considering these statistics we must of course take into account the fact that five of the fourteen emendations are for two lines of text. Comment on this segment has not been exhausted, but I see no further emendations to make, and therefore it will be useful to turn to other examples. These are chosen not to represent a cross-section, if that were possible, but to provide to the subject a short supplemental introduction, one somewhat more conservative.

'airs' read 'avis' (511.20): To the *FW* galleys Joyce added, among other esoteric materials, two patches of Lithuanian words, drawn from his notes in Buffalo Ms. VI. B. 46. From the note 'avis (sheep) oska (goat)' he composed a phrase for the second of the patches and inserted as follows: ', as avis said to oska,' (B.M. Add. Ms. 47487. 212). The typist copied ',as airs said to oska,' on –.211b, the back of the preceding galley sheet. (An advantage of examples taken from these galleys is that we may all but infallibly rule out the possibility of intermediate Mss. or Tss.) Though 'avis' and 'airs' do not much look alike in print, they are quite similar in script, particularly this Joyce script with its pointed 'v'. The typist read the ligature between 'v' and 'i' as the roof of an 'r' and assumed the jot – actually perfectly in place – to belong with the first stroke of the 'v'.

'Siker' read 'Siku' (237.31): Similarly, two patches of Kiswahili were added, drawn from his notes in the same notebook. From the note 'siku (day)' he composed a sentence for the second of the patches and added as follows: 'Siku of calmy days.' (B.M. Add. Ms. 47477.283). The typist copied 'Siker of calmy days.' on –.282b, the back of the preceding galley sheet. The 'u' Joyce wrote was sloppy, with suggestions of loops in the minims; the first was read as 'e', the second followed as 'r'.

'chepachap' read 'chapachap' (237.15): From the note 'barna (letter), chapa (stamp)' in this notebook Joyce composed a phrase for the same patch of Kiswahili and inserted as follows: ', our barnaboy, our chapachap,' (B.M. Add. Ms. 47477.283). The typist copied 'our barneboy, our chepachap,' on –.282b, the back of the preceding galley sheet. 'barneboy' was corrected but 'chepachap' missed. The typist's error, one of the most common ones, was the same in both cases, the misreading of 'a' as 'e'.[18]

'an sable' read 'au sable' (199.18): On rare occasions it is possible to discover and emend a mistake without recourse to manuscripts. These two words were added to *Anna Livia Plurabelle* at a stage when few changes were made not involving rivers. What Joyce added here was the river Au Sable of Michigan. The printer, influenced by 'ansable' in a typescript of the manuscript changes in his galleys (Buffalo), read the 'u' as 'n'. Of all minim letters, these two are of course the most difficult to distinguish in an unknown handwritten context. I have recently unearthed galley proofs for the Gaige edition (1928) in which 'au sable' was added and then incorrectly set, but obviously nothing can finally be proven by reference to them: the problem can be solved only by explication, i.e., by establishing the context. It is in fact to point up the importance of explication that this example is given. Joyce's late hand is not for the most part such as to make the rough places plain, but a good deal rougher, and no matter how intensively it is analyzed it cannot be read well, when at all, in ignorance of the material it records.

'ethur:' read 'ethur!' (349.5): The autograph exclamation mark (B.M. Add. Ms. 47480.31b) was transmitted correctly through at least two typescripts (–.53 and –.92) but was set as a colon by the *transition* printer (–.120, –.141). This error was facilitated by three circumstances. First, here – as in almost all *FW* typescripts which I can bring to mind – the exclamation mark was made with two strokes, period plus apostrophe, the apostrophe, as usual, in the shape of a comma. This made a rather odd exclamation mark at best, but, secondly, it is a peculiarity of the typescripts in question that all periods appeared in an elevated position, their centers being on an average slightly over half-minim height. The resulting exclamation mark occurred dozens of times and was therefore thoroughly familiar to the printer by the time he set 'marsh!' and 'zimmerminnes!' in the two sentences preceding, but a third circumstance, which allowed him to consider the strange but identical mark in isolation, was the nature of the sentence and its position. Assuming thought, conscious or otherwise, it seems that the printer expected to follow, at whatever distance, the song to be sung. Certainly the reader must expect something to follow the colon, song or otherwise, and since there is nothing, the structure of Taff's speech, of the page, and ultimately of the entire episode is brought into question.

insert comma after 'Isad' and for 'gag' read 'gay' (580.18): To *FW* galley sheet B.M. Add. Ms. 47487.122 Joyce added between 'slumbwhere,' and 'flispering' a passage beginning 'till' and ending 'and gentle Isad, Ysut gay,'. Only the closing words are treated here. In copying these onto –.121b, the back of the preceding galley sheet, the typist made two mistakes: the 'd' of 'Isad' was typed on the edge of the sheet, so that the comma fell on the typewriter's roller,[19] and 'gay' was typed 'gag'. The latter error is ironic, for while Joyce's 'g's and 'y's were frequently close enough to be confused, no confusion could have occurred here except that the tip of the pen was almost dry as the first stroke was made: the outline is faint, but distinct to the careful eye. We realize here in the most immediate terms the incalculable damage which can be done the text by the smallest changes. This pair destroyed sense, syntax, rhythm, sound, and appearance, the counterpoint of '-sad' and 'gay' and the succession they form with 'gentle'. '. . . and gentle Isad, Ysut gay, flispering in the nightleaves flattery, dinsiduously, to Finnegan . . .'

Of the more than 600 emendations in hand at the time of writing, not every one, of course, is as choice as these, but it must be evident that all corruptions of the text are important, and that in the final analysis they are equally so: it is the nature of *Finnegans Wake* that every particle of its text tells a tale. All corruptions whatever alter the appearance of the text, all but a handful alter its sound, and their deadly effects rarely fail to extend to profounder levels.

Now, how could the text be corrupt to such an extent? As Leon Kellner wrote in *Restoring Shakespeare* (Knopf, 1925), 'When we have the "Barrack Room Ballads" before us with the name of Rudyard Kipling as the author on the title page, we are perfectly safe to assume that Mr. Kipling handed over the poems to his publishers, that he went through the proof-sheets, and saw to it that no serious misprints were left. The names of the author and the publishers guarantee that.' We should be safe in assuming as much about *Finnegans Wake*—Joyce even read the book as published and made hundreds of further corrections and revisions—yet I hope to demonstrate to the dismayed satisfaction of all that *Finnegans Wake* is actually squarely in a class with the Shakespearean texts rather than *Barrack-Room Ballads*. Given the nature of the book and the circumstances of its composition, this should occasion us no great surprise. There exists no text remotely comparable to it in complexity. It passed through stage after stage after stage of addition and revision and the mechanical processes intervened at early points. The typists were often dazzlingly incompetent—what less can be said of anyone typing characters onto the roller of their machine, for instance?—and of course the printers did their bit when publishing and republishing the bulk of the book in periodicals and as small books, though luckily the skillful Scottish printers who set the complete text were exceedingly careful and introduced few errors. The inevitable confusion could have been kept within certain limits had Joyce not been handicapped from the start by varying degrees of blindness. What vision he had he spent largely in further composition: he was creator rather than clerk. However cherished the notion that were 'airs', 'gag', etc., really errors he would surely have seen at least most of them, it must fall before the mass of evidence I will advance. But another notion will be longer in yielding to reason, viz., that Joyce delighted in accidentals.

What is mainly wrong with this cliché is that it fails to discriminate among various types of accidentals. Indeed, outside of convergence and similar phenomena of languages, and history, etc., and several documented cases in which Joyce deliberately used misprints and other errors from sources, it is not possible to prove a delight in accidentals at all,[20] and when by accidentals we mean misprints, it is possible to prove nothing but concern. Certainly it would have been paradoxical for a writer who approached language with an unheard-of precision to be delighted by thousands of corrupting changes in a text to whose laborious and painstaking construction he had devoted almost a third of his lifetime. Why should he have ransacked the Lithuanian language for such words as 'avis' and 'oska' and with them have composed phrases of such elemental lucidity, were it only to be 'delighted' in the end with gibberish? It is up to the purveyors of such novel doctrines to establish them as respectable positions: nothing of the kind has been attempted. It is from this preposterous quarter that we must particularly beware the sophistical argument. As Bowers writes in *Textual and Literary Criticism* (Cambridge, 1959), 'It is a true remark of Sir Walter Greg's that often more misplaced ingenuity is devoted to defending a wrong reading than to emending it.'[21] Thus in the case of 'airs' someone will admit it an accidental change but insist that Joyce saw and approved of it, for 'airs' is almost an anagram of Aries, the Ram, and since avis meant sheep . . . To point out that this is lunacy, pure and simple, is of little or no use in the present state of *Wake* studies, but that does not prevent one proceeding to do one's work. I find the text less than perfect, and I have determined to carry out a textual critique, to result commonly in emendation. This task entails systematic analyses of all known and discoverable extant material, upwards of 20,000 pages, of which the majority are atrociously difficult even to decipher, but it is a task which can and will be accomplished in time. I think it a task eminently worthy of all the erudition and passion which can be brought to it, for the understanding of this endlessly fascinating book depends upon it.

NOTES

1 Originally simply 'Kevin'. (Material from the manuscripts used with permission of the Estate; in the case of Buffalo manuscripts, with the additional permission of the Lockwood Memorial Library of the University)

2 Originally 'pious Kevin'. In the next draft Joyce inserted a non-pattern 'Kevin' following this: it survives at 605.18

3 A note of this series is found in Buffalo Ms. VI. E. 25: 'Kevineen (9 names)'. (The numbers imposed on the Buffalo notebooks are in effect arbitrary, often absurd as here, but they must be used for at least the time being as a means of identification)

4 'whiteclad' (605.6) yields white, 'arose' (-.10) rose, 'cloth of gold' (-.-) gold, 'Glendalough-le-vert' (-.11) green, 'rubric' (-.23) red, 'violet' (606.4) violet,

'sable' (−.5) black. There are said to be officially only five liturgical colors: white, red, green, violet, black. However, rose is traditionally used on Laetare and Gaudete Sundays; and cloth of gold may be substituted for red, white, and green, cloth of silver for white. The first source I consulted, a missal commonly used in the United States, listed seven colors in its introduction to the liturgy, omitting only silver, which is so like white as hardly to be distinctive. Joyce inserts rose and gold after white and transposes red and green in the order of colors given in the *Catholic Encyclopedia*

5 wisdom (606.6–7), understanding (−.1), counsel (605.28), fortitude (−.24), knowledge (−.18), piety (−.13), and the fear of the Lord (604.27–8). This is the order—which Joyce uses in reverse—found in the *Catholic Encyclopedia* and in Isaiah 11 : 2–3 (Douay). The last gift is found outside the episode proper in an introductory sentence which, until 1938, was only two lines long, not thirteen as now: the passages between 'filial fearer,' and 'the miracles' were late additions. The separation as it first appeared was only slightly anomalous, and possibly was based on Isaiah, which gives the first six of these gifts in verse 2 and the fear of the Lord in verse 3. I don't believe Joyce was at all aware of pushing the fear of the Lord so far out of the pattern. One addition to the paragraph included the word 'knowledge' (604.32), certainly an inadvertence

6 Many intricacies are not germane to this study but may be partially examined here. Most remarkable, I think, is the number of interlocked words, this category including pairs of opposites: 'Procreated', 'precreated', 'postcreated', 'concreated', and 'recreated', 'on' and 'in', 'come' and 'came', 'celibate matrimony', 'westfrom' and 'eastward', '-from went and came . . . to', 'river Yssia and Essia river', 'centripetally' and 'ventrifugal', 'subject' and 'supreem', 'Yshgafiena and Yshgafiuna', 'proceded' and 'receded', 'gregorian' and 'ambrosian' (the two kinds of R.C. chants), 'effused' and 'affusion', 'water' and 'dry land', '*insularis*' and 'universal', 'memory' and 'intellect', '*extempore*' and 'formally', and 'proposing' and 'considering' are most of them. With the first group belong 'Increate' and 'Creator' (604.27: see note 5 for explanation of their separation from the episode, and see the end of this note for emendation of 'Increate' from 'increate'). Among these belong also the two feasts of the True Cross, the Invention and the Exaltation (605.9). I have noted only one other group, poverty (605.7), chastity (606.1), and obedience (605.29), a three. I should mention the beehive hut enclosures of ancient Ireland (605.24), since these are not common knowledge, but the remaining religious imagery and diction ought to be left for the pleasure of the reader. To sum up, this degree of complexity bears comparison with the knottiest parts of the book, yet except for a small handful of odd spellings ('ysland', 'pravilege', etc.) and neologisms ('westfrom', etc.) the episode could be taken as a passage of pure, single-level English. As always, Joyce chose the texture he wished to achieve. It was not one imposed on him by his materials

'increate' read 'Increate' (604.27): 'Increate' and 'Creator' were added to 'God' and 'Lord' at the same time the other *create* words were added (seven in all). Their capital initials disappeared with the rest in the second typescript (see note 14). 'Creator' was restored apparently through the typist's misreading of her copy, in which 'c' was struck over a 'd', suggesting to her eye a capital letter (B.M. Add. Ms. 47488.37 and −.57). 'Increate' must now be restored. It is not a mere adjective, but part of the name (noun). 'Increate God' and 'the Lord

Creator' are parallel, as are 'the servant' and 'a filial fearer' following them. The capital 'I' is necessary to the sense, of which this parallelism is part

7 298.L2: *Ecclesiastical and Celestial Hierarchies. The Ascending. The Descending.*
Emendation of '*Ecclasiastical*': '*Ecclasiastical*' added to typescript in an extremely poor and messy hand (B.M. Add. Ms. 47478.77), typed '*Ecclasiastical*' (–.108), and so persisted. Joyce's typists were of course all at sea, and it depended on the moment as to which of a number of disparate tendencies would assert itself. In one case a pun would revert to straight English, but much more frequently the typists were willing to write out any sequence of letters whatever, and given the nature of the book, the expectation is more outraged by straight English than by distortion. This is my comment on the problem of why anyone given a chance of copying '*Ecclesiastical*' should instead write '*Ecclasiastical*'. The classical rule of *lectio difficilior* must be applied to *FW* with the most extreme caution

8 Thus R.C. terminology and the Douay Bible (Col. 1 : 16), after the Vulgate's 'dominationes'. King James gives the more familiar 'dominions'. Understandably, Joyce tended in such matters to follow his Roman training

9 Note that Joyce specifies sext to fall at noon. Modern R.C. practice often makes it earlier, but for Joyce's purposes – the reasons are obvious – twelve o'clock is the proper time at a center. It is of interest that in the list from which Joyce copied the hours, marking out with blue crayon as he went, 'Sext' is unmarked (Buffalo Ms. VI. B. 25). I believe we can assume, then, that 'Sext' was used last, with more deliberation, as coupled with the Eucharist and standing in a fixed relationship to the other cross and the center of the episode

10 A further defense against the intermediate draft theory is the *reductio ad absurdum*: to explain away my work we should eventually have postulated an almost complete set of intermediate drafts and its systematic disappearance. This point is very important, for while it is possible to demonstrate the existence of things visible, it is impossible to prove – in the fullest sense of that word – the nonexistence of invisible nothings

11 The syntactical problem is of necessity simplified at this point

12 Included in this count is the first Kevin typescript made by Harriet Weaver in 1923, apparently now lost

13 The words 'and Glendalough' were added as an afterthought, which accounts for the awkward construction of this sentence

14 Miss Weaver's typescript was apparently all caps – such typescripts were commonly made because of the state of Joyce's eyes – without initial cap underlinings, for this one came out lower case except for the first 'Kevin', 'God', 'Lord', 'Ireland' and an odd 'Arch-angelical' (survived to galley proof) and 'Cardinal'

15 'center' persisted through the two following typescripts, through the galley proofs, and into the (missing) page proofs. Joyce's correction is found on –.238: 'Page 606 line 3 from top instead of "center" read "centre"'

16 All of the names are pompous and comical in their involuted redundancies. It is interesting to observe in passing the note from which Joyce drew the altar aspect: 'Fr Bern Vaughan granted privilege of portable altar' (Buffalo Ms. VI. B. 10.13; *FW* 605.7–8, 'having been graunted the pravilege of a priest's post-created portable *altare cum balneo*'). This Father Bernard Vaughan was to Joyce a figure of fun, whose 'enormities' he followed with delight in the press

17 'Textual Criticism' in *The Aims and Methods of Scholarship in Modern Languages and Literatures*, ed. James Thorpe (New York: Modern Language Association of America, 1963), p. 32

18 To facilitate exposition, one datum in the foregoing was falsified: what Joyce had correctly entered in his notes was 'barua (letter)' but the 'u' was so totally ambiguous that he later read 'barna' and made it the basis, through 'barn', of the compound 'barnaboy'. In meaning and sound the mistake is written immutably into the text. This account assumes only that his source, unknown, was correct, so that for 'barna' Joyce was unwittingly his own source. In any case, 'barna-' is incorrect. Similarly, mistakes were caused by amanuenses. In the rear of notebook VI. B. 22 there is entered, in the hand of an amanuensis, an extensive French-Flemish vocabulary. Some years later the unused parts of the notebook were copied out by another amanuensis, Mme France Raphael, and it was this list which Joyce used. Mme Raphael had corrupted the correct original note 'oreiller–oorkussen' to 'oreiller–oerkussen', therefore 'oerkussens' at 393.32. More common were mistakes in printed sources. From the 1923 edition of Bartholomew's *Handy Reference Atlas of the World* Joyce culled a 'Jurna' River, which he made to serve as 'journey' in the sentence 'So save to jurna's end!' (215.8–9); unfortunately, a Jurna never flowed: it is the Jurua. Neither is there, outside Bartholomew's, a 'Souldre' River (202.14); it is the Sauldre. The incorrect version serves in the text as 'soldier', a task it might not have been given as 'Sauldre'. Such frustrating specimens are luckily few in number. They must be isolated, but since they are textually correct, their isolation is not properly the business of a textual critique. It is axiomatic that mistakes attributable to Joyce's sources can never be corrected. Keats's 'stout Cortez' is the type of this class of error

19 In the galleys prepared for the printer part of the 'd' was typed off the side of the sheet, so that if the comma had not disappeared in first typescript it would have disappeared here (–.269b)

20 E.g.: In a notebook of the middle twenties Joyce wrote ' $\wedge$c on vibrating bed'. The symbol keyed the phrase for use in the third watch of Shaun (III.3), but it did not find its place there. Years later, in the thirties, the unused contents of this notebook were copied by the amanuensis Mme Raphael. At this point she wrote '$\wedge$ convibrating bed', which Joyce made the basis of 'convibrational bed' at 394.3–4. It is good enough for our present purposes to say that more than a decade separated the original note and its eventual use. There is no reason to suppose that Joyce remembered his note after all this time or that he doubted the authenticity of Mme Raphael's version. The only thing which can be proven is that he used her version

21 Kellner, also, remarked 'the obstinacy of conservative editors and particularly commentators to whom the printed text is inviolable, and who will explain anything rather than admit a printer's error'. These dicta are in reference to Shakespearean editing, which must attempt to reconstruct its manuscripts. It must be understood that there is no question of 'misplaced ingenuity' in saying that 'airs' is a misreading of 'avis'. We have the manuscripts and we know it to be a fact. Our only concern in the case is whether Joyce saw and approved of the wreckage. This is where 'misplaced ingenuity' impinges on *Finnegans Wake* editing

It is convenient in this context to make another distinction, concerning the technical word 'conjectural'. This term is used by bibliographers in connection with readings for which there is no known extant documentary evidence. It is of necessity used constantly in Shakespearean editing. Very very few of my *FW* emendations will be conjectural. Almost always the problem is choice between variants (there are rarely more than two)

REFERENCES

The following texts are quoted and cited in this book:

Stephen Hero, New York: New Directions, 1944, 1955, and London: Jonathan Cape, 1944. The first English edition is used simply because it was the only one available at the time of editing.

A Portrait of the Artist as a Young Man, New York: Viking Press, 1964, and London: Jonathan Cape, 1956. The new American edition was prepared by Chester G. Anderson and arbitrated by Richard Ellmann. It is on its face superior to all other editions, and it may prove 'definitive'. The 1956 Cape edition is used because it is current, though its text is undoubtedly less accurate than previous English editions, being reset.

Ulysses, New York: Random House, 1961, and London: The Bodley Head, 1960. The current editions are the most corrupt ever printed, excepting the first printing of the first edition and pirates and their descendants. The American edition has a few more errors but is infinitely preferable to the English, which mutilates Joyce's format–principally in *Circe*. The 1960 edition is cited only because it is current.

Finnegans Wake, London: Faber & Faber, 1939, and New York: Viking Press, 1939. The text quoted and cited is my copy of the first English trade edition, which has been corrected by collation with Buffalo Mss. VI. H. 4. a. and b. For the quotations and citations in this volume it is apparently identical in text and lineation with other editions and need not be further described here. A forthcoming paper will treat it fully. It is hoped that quotation of the text will be perfectly accurate so that the reader may identify one silent change, which will be covered later by an emendation.

In each case the edition listed first is the basis for quotation. Except for *Finnegans Wake*, citation is by means of two numbers, the second enclosed in brackets and referring to the editions listed second above.

EDITOR

THE CONTRIBUTORS

These brief notes mention, with other information, each contributor's major publications in the Joyce field and/or major publications related in subject to his present essay.

PADRAIC COLUM: New York and Dublin. Co-author of *Our Friend James Joyce*, contributed, among other introductions, that to the Crosby Gaige *Anna Livia Plurabelle* (1928).

FRANK BUDGEN: London. Author of *James Joyce and the Making of Ulysses*, one of twelve contributors to *Our Exagmination Round His Factification for Incamination of Work in Progress* (1929).

FREDERICK J. HOFFMAN: University of Wisconsin, Milwaukee. Author of *Freudianism and the Literary Mind*, which includes a chapter on Joyce.

VIVIAN MERCIER: University of Colorado. Author of *The Irish Comic Tradition*.

FRITZ SENN: Zürich. A professional proofreader. Co-editor (with Clive Hart) of *A Wake Newslitter*, author of articles and notes on Joyce.

ROBERT F. GLECKNER: University of California, Riverside. Author of a forthcoming study of Byron's non-satiric poetry, co-editor of *Romanticism: Points of View*, author and editor of three Blake books, two forthcoming.

JAMES S. ATHERTON: Wigan Technical College, Lancs. Author of *The Books at the Wake*, contributed editorial matter for 1964 Heinemann edition of *Portrait*.

J. MITCHELL MORSE: Penn State University. Author of *The Sympathetic Alien: James Joyce and Catholicism*.

NATHAN HALPER: New York City and Provincetown. A dealer in art. Author of several wellknown articles on Joyce.

THE CONTRIBUTORS

RICHARD M. KAIN: University of Louisville. Author of *Fabulous Voyager: James Joyce's Ulysses, Dublin in the Age of William Butler Yeats and James Joyce*, co-author of *Joyce: the Man, the Work, the Reputation*, co-editor of *The Workshop of Daedalus*.

A. WALTON LITZ: Princeton University. Author of *The Art of James Joyce*.

DAVID HAYMAN: University of Iowa. Editor of *A First-Draft Version of Finnegans Wake*, author of *Joyce et Mallarmé*.

JACK P. DALTON: Buffalo. Recipient of a Guggenheim Fellowship (1964–65) for work towards an edition of sixtysix notebooks used in the composition of *Finnegans Wake*, author of a forthcoming monograph on the text of *Ulysses*.

EDITORIAL AFTERWORD

'to day 16 of June 1924 | twenty years after. | Will anybody remember | this date' (Buffalo Ms. VI. B. 5, p. 39). When Joyce dictated these words to Nora he was lying in Dr Borsch's clinic in the first stages of recovering from an especially unpleasant iridectomy, performed on the 11th. Before the operation he had been in a 'state of dejection' and was afterwards depressed.

Joyce was keen on anniversaries and would have been pleased by those of 1964 – the 60th of Bloomsday, the 50th of *Portrait*, the 25th of *Finnegans Wake*. He himself, born in 1882, would have celebrated his 82nd birthday. This collection of essays originated in the desire to do something special to mark the 25th anniversary of the publication of *Finnegans Wake*. We hope that Joyce would have been further pleased by this gesture and its substance. Certainly he ought to have been gratified that the collection, of its own will, turned out a dodecade – it was his plan, of course, that *Our Exagmination Round His Factification for Incamination of Work in Progress* (1929) should contain twelve essays, matching one of the groups of the *Wake*, the twelve men who appear in many guises – and certainly he ought to have been gratified by the presence of two of his closest friends, Padraic Colum and Frank Budgen, Mr Budgen one of the 1929 exagminators.

At the beginning, I didn't feel inclined to seeing the book through by myself, so I enlisted the help of Clive Hart. He was responsible for most of the solicitation which brought in the essays accepted, but since he has not been further associated with the book, it would be unfair to blame him for any faults which may be found. In preparing the essays for publication I have taken a broad view of editorial responsibility. In only a few particulars has a uniform style been imposed on the contributors, but considerable time and effort were spent in assuring accuracy of the data, for, except in some cases in which it seemed impractical, I checked the facts. I hope that this reversal of the typical editorial role will give satisfaction.

The essays were especially prepared for this volume and all appear here for the first time, with these two reservations: Mr Mercier's essay, without notes and otherwise different, was read at the 1950 MLA meeting at the University of Wisconsin, Madison, and a good deal of the St Kevin material in my own essay is reworked from two articles which appeared in the *James Joyce Quarterly* in 1964.

The tilly, Padraic Colum's elegy, appeared first in his recent *Irish Elegies* (Dublin, The Dolmen Press), entitled 'The Artificer'. It was 'produced immediately on the announcement of death', as Mr Colum wrote of the elegies in a preface. Several slight changes were made by the poet for this publication. It is a great pleasure to bring the elegy to the attention of Joyceans.

The frontispiece is a portrait made by Ruth Asch. I prefer it to all others except one, and this one, made at the same sitting, would be the frontispiece had I been able to locate a satisfactory copy. I have found it in three states. It appeared on a poster advertising the Odyssey Press *Ulysses*, but overprinted and copy badly worn along the folds. It appeared on a poster advertising the 1930 Rhein-Verlag *Ulysses*, but copies badly worn along the folds. There is a slip proof of the portrait, autographed in 1929, but covered by some thoughtful person with deep gouges and other markings. Rhein-Verlag informs me that all of its copies of the portrait were destroyed in Munich during the war. Ruth Asch is apparently not to be found in Berlin. I suspect that the portraits were made at the instance of Rhein-Verlag and that it took all copies of the one it considered best, for Joyce was able to give Sylvia Beach original prints of four or five other portraits made at the sitting but only a slip proof of this one. There are further possibilities for search, and a satisfactory copy may yet be found. It is, however, a very keen pleasure indeed to use this present portrait as frontispiece. It is reproduced by courtesy of the Lockwood Memorial Library, Buffalo.

I acknowledge gratefully that I did almost all of my share in this book while enjoying a Fellowship of the John Simon Guggenheim Memorial Foundation. In particular, I owe to the Fellowship the notebook materials in my 'Advertisement'.

J. P. D.

Buffalo, New York
July 5, 1965